FOREST
PENJING

FOREST PENJING

Enjoy the Miniature Landscape by Growing, Care and Appreciation of Chinese Bonsai Trees

BY ZHAO QINGQUAN
Translated by ZHAO GANG

丛林盆景

SCPG

Copyright © 2022 Shanghai Press and Publishing Development Co., Ltd.

This book is edited and designed by the Editorial Committee of *Cultural China* series.

Text by Zhao Qingquan
Photographs by Zhao Qingquan, Wu Chengfa, Zheng Yongtai, Han Xuenian, Zhang Zhigang, Zhou Qijin, Liu Shaohong, Fan Yicheng, Huang Le, and Lu Zengqiang
Foreword by Lindsay Bebb
Translation by Zhao Gang
Cover Design by Wang Wei
Interior Design by Li Jing, Hu Bin (Yuan Yinchang Design Studio)

Copy Editor: Nicholas Choa
Editor: Wu Yuezhou
Editorial Director: Zhang Yicong

ISBN: 978-1-93836-857-8

Address any comments about *Forest Penjing: Enjoy the Miniature Landscape by Growing, Care and Appreciation of Chinese Bonsai Trees* to:

SCPG
401 Broadway, Ste. 1000
New York, NY 10013
USA

or

Shanghai Press and Publishing Development Co., Ltd.
390 Fuzhou Road, Shanghai, China (200001)
Email: sppdbook@163.com

Printed in China by Shanghai Donnelley Printing Co., Ltd.

1   3   5   7   9   10   8   6   4   2

CONTENTS

On page 1
Fig. 1   Please refer to fig. 171 on page 102.

On pages 2–3
Fig. 2   Please refer to fig. 174 on page 103.

On facing page
Fig. 3   Please refer to fig. 84 on page 55.

CONTENTS

On facing page
Fig. 4   Please refer to fig. 154 on page 96.

FOREWORD

前言

I first met Zhao Qingquan at the 2nd World Bonsai Convention in Florida, USA in 1993 after winning a chance to see his huge penjing landscape demonstration of Chinese elms in the convention raffle with just 2 tickets! Prior to that, I had never seen him demonstrate live, but I was already very familiar with his excellent penjing creations.

Zhao Qingquan has been a great master of penjing works within China since 1985 and has been demonstrating and promoting penjing extensively both inside and outside China since 1988.

He has made an enormous contribution to the understanding of penjing outside China, not only through his demonstrations, but also through his several books on penjing published in English.

This book, *Forest Penjing*, is again a brilliant work. It explains in simple to understand dialogue, the different types of forest penjing and how to create and display them. Chapter III of the book outlines the many factors that need to be considered in the creation of forest penjing and is not only thought provoking, but in itself provides both relaxation and energy during the creation process. I think that considering all of these factors while creating a forest penjing will make the experience much more rewarding, especially if the creator can employ most of them in one creation. Zhao Qingquan also supports his instruction with wonderful examples of forest penjing.

I am sure that if you follow the principles Zhao outlines in this book, you will not only thoroughly enjoy the creation process, but will also have a marvellous forest penjing to live with in your garden.

Lindsay Bebb
Chairman
World Bonsai Friendship Federation

On facing page

Fig. 5 *Golden Autumn*

Tree species: diamond-leaf persimmon
Tree height: 100 cm
Designer: Lu Zengqiang

Persimmon trees of varied heights growing out of the same root are planted in a shallow pot with good density and placement priority. This work depicts a standard forest.

Fig. 6 Beauty of the flower: the flowering quince.

PREFACE

Penjing, which originated in ancient China, has a history of more than a thousand years. Taking plants, rocks, soil, and water as its main materials and combining horticulture, craft production, and artistic creation, penjing exhibits the beauty of nature in pots.

Penjing is the advanced stage in the development of potted gardening. It condenses the scenery of the universe into a small pot and expresses artistic beauty and human emotion. It is a plastic, malleable art form, jointly created by man and nature.

Penjing possesses a natural beauty unparalleled by artificial works of art, as well as a natural charm lacking in many other works of the plastic arts, because its major materials are plants and rocks, which are precisely what it exhibits. The plants display the vital signs of nature, which change with the passing of the seasons.

Chinese penjing, based on the objects it manifests and the different materials it uses, can be divided into three types: tree penjing, landscape penjing, and water and land penjing. Tree penjing, which is known internationally as *penzai* (potted plants) or by its Japanese name, bonsai, uses woody plants as its main materials and focuses on the depiction of trees, with the composition's dominant elements shaped through wiring, pruning, and carving. Landscape penjing depicts a miniature landscape by carefully selecting and shaping

rocks, which are usually placed in a shallow container in contact with water. Water and land penjing effectively combines the first two types and is itself a unique type of penjing in China. It depicts natural scenery in a comprehensive way by using plants, rocks, soil, water, and sometimes small ornaments as well.

When three or more trees are arranged in a tree penjing or a water and land penjing, it is called a forest penjing, which can take the form of a thicket or a dense forest.

Forest penjing can generally be broken down into four types based on structure: the multiple-tree forest formed by no less than three independent trees artistically arranged in the same container, the multiple-tree forest with roots interconnected, the forest consisting of a single tree with multiple trunks, and the crouching single-trunk forest formed by one tree lying on the ground with branches growing out of its trunk.

Of the different types of penjing, forest penjing possesses the strongest vital energy, forms the most striking contrast, and offers the most realistic impression of nature. It is also the most capable of presenting poetic and picturesque scenes and demonstrating the creator's artistic cultivation. It can be considered a garden in miniature. When we view a fine work of penjing at home over a cup of tea with peace of mind, we may feel as if we were in nature amidst the tranquility of mountain forests, listening to a gurgling stream and chirping birds.

Materials for forest penjing are easily accessible. Trees can be obtained through

On facing page
Fig. 7   Please refer to fig. 155 on page 96.

artificial breeding, which is low in cost and biologically friendly. There are no strict requirements for the age, thickness, and shape of the trees. Many trees, when viewed independently, may be imperfect, but with careful organization, they can still create a fine overall effect. Therefore, in the creation of forest penjing, there is relatively little restriction of materials and the artist can give full play to his or her artistic creativity.

Forest penjing as an art form was present in ancient China. As early as the Ming dynasty (1368–1644), forest penjing appeared in books and paintings. Nowadays, forest penjing can be found in a variety of exhibitions, both within China and abroad. The emergence of more and more excellent works fully displays the value of forest penjing.

I have always loved forest penjing and as an experienced penjing maker, I have thought about this art form in great depth. Therefore, in this book, I would like to share with the reader my decades of insight into and experience of making forest penjing. My wish is that more and more people will love and value this unique art form and help it reach new heights.

Supplemented with pictures, this book systematically introduces forest penjing, including its appreciation, categorization, production, maintenance, and display. I also include many examples for the reader's reference.

Zhao Qingquan
June 2020

Fig. 8 *The Wind Blows*
Tree species: five-needle pine
Type of rock: Yingde stone
Container length: 120 cm
Designer: Zhao Qingquan

This is a work depicting a water and land forest. The rocks separate the water from the land. Trees grow on the land alongside the water.

CHAPTER I
THE BEAUTY OF FOREST PENJING

Fig. 10   Beauty of the root: the trident maple.

Penjing can be viewed as the sculpture of natural scenes. Jointly created by man and nature, it is an art form that combines natural beauty and artistic beauty, the two aspects for which penjing is appreciated.

1. Natural and Ecological Beauty

Trees are the main materials for forest penjing. They possess not only natural forms and colors, but also vital signs and natural charm. Therefore, a forest penjing made of trees is like a living work of art, exhibiting a relationship between plants that mirrors that of a natural forest. The work changes with the growth of the trees and presents different scenes with the alteration of the seasons, making viewers feel as if they were right at the source. Realistic and overflowing with the energy of nature, these works exhibit natural and ecological beauty.

The vital signs of forest penjing determine that the creation of penjing is a process of continuity. Unlike a work of painting or sculpture which, once completed, requires no further changes, a forest penjing usually cannot be completed once and for all but needs continuous effort because the trees keep growing and changing. Some works may not be satisfying now, but as the plants grow, they may improve with time. But, on the other hand, they may also lose their desired shape. Therefore, continuity in creation is a special charm of the penjing art form, because it can fill viewers with boundless expectations.

The natural and ecological beauty of forest penjing is embodied not only in the beauty of the root, trunk, branch, leaf, flower, and fruit, but also in the beauty of the community of trees, changing of the seasons, and different kinds of forests.

Beauty of the Root: Some roots stretch in all directions, solid and stable; some rise up high, revealing themselves in the air; some intertwine with the roots of other trees, forming an organic whole; some have plants growing out of them, forming a grove; some penetrate cracks in rocks, struggling to survive in a harsh environment (fig. 10). They come in varied forms, each displaying their own unique beauty.

On pages 14–15

Fig. 9   *In the Depth of the Shade*

Tree species: Chinese elm
Type of rock: turtle grain stone
Container length: 120 cm
Designer: Meng Guangling

In this water and land penjing, the trunks are hard and the branches are soft; the soil and rocks are hard and the water is soft. The work is a pleasing combination of hardness and softness.

Fig. 11   Beauty of the trunk: the five-needle pine.

Fig. 12   Beauty of the branch: the Chinese sweet plum.

Fig. 13   Beauty of the leaf: the Japanese maple.

Beauty of the Trunk: Trunks come in a diverse range of shapes. Some grow straight up, vigorous and tall; some lean in a certain direction, displaying great momentum; some are gracefully twisted, rich in variety; some combine all the aforementioned shapes, displaying unity in diversity. In addition, different species of trees have different kinds of bark. Some are covered all over with scales, some feel smooth and delicate, and some possess a primitive simplicity. Different trunks also have different colors; some of the common colors are yellowish-brown, ash black, dark red, dark green, and greyish white (fig. 11).

Beauty of the Branch: Branches vary with different tree species. Some are upright and expansive, some are twisted and revolving, some are vigorous, thick, and scattered, some are gently crooked and dense, some grow upwards like buckhorns, and some lower their heads like crab claws (fig. 12).

Beauty of the Leaf: This is mainly on display in the shape, color, and texture of the leaf. The leaf is often shaped like a needle, a scale, an oval, a palm, or a fan. The colors are usually light green, dark green, yellowish green, and red violet. Some even have a colorful edge or are patterned. Leaves can be thick or thin, hard or soft (fig. 13).

Beauty of the Flower: Flowers are more diverse in shape and color, displaying a rich variety of forms (see fig. 6 on page 9). The shape of a flower varies with different tree species. The colors are usually dark red, pink, purple, yellow, light green, or white. Some tree species may have flowers of different colors on the same branch.

Beauty of the Fruit: Fruits used for forest penjing are generally small and beautiful. They may be round, oval, cone-shaped, or gourd-shaped. Their colors include red, yellow, purple, orange, green and black (fig. 14).

Fig. 14   Beauty of the fruit: the pomegranate.

Fig. 15 *A Tranquil Forest*

Tree species: Chinese elm
Type of rock: turtle grain stone
Container length: 70 cm
Designer: Zhao Qingquan

The trees are luxuriant, appropriate in height, and in picturesque disorder. They compete yet live in harmony, embodying the communal beauty of natural forests.

Beauty of the Community of Trees:
In forest penjing, the different parts of a tree may combine to form integrated beauty. Moreover, all the trees used are arranged according to the rule of natural ecology. They simultaneously compete and live in harmony, embodying the beauty of the whole and authentically reflecting the existence of life in nature to the fullest. This is unparalleled in other forms of penjing (fig. 15).

Beauty of Seasonal Change: As they grow, the trees in forest penjing may change in posture, color, and charm according to the passing of the seasons. This is especially true of forest penjing consisting of miscellaneous trees. They are tender green in spring, deeply shaded in summer, golden yellow in autumn, and desolate and lonesome in winter. The seasonal characteristics of forest penjing that contain flowers and fruit are even more evident. The beauty of seasonal change reflected in forest penjing is much greater than that present in other forms of penjing. It is thus of immense pleasure to watch the growth of the trees in forest penjing (fig. 16).

Beauty of Different Kinds of Forests:
Forest penjing can display different kinds of
forests in different ecological environments,
such as forests in open country, in mountains,
by water, along streams, on islands, along
the seashore, in swamps, in deserts, and in
tropical regions. The diverse scenes they
embody enable the viewer to experience the
pleasure of travel without going outdoors
(fig. 17 and see fig. 18 on pages 20 and 21).

Fig. 16 *Ancient Trees by a Clear Pond*
Tree species: Chinese elm
Type of rock: turtle grain stone
Container length: 150 cm
Designer: Zhao Qingquan

Chinese elms in winter, with all their leaves fallen,
display unique charm. When covered with silver-
white snow, they show the beauty of seasonal change.

Fig. 17 *Idyllic Country Life*
Tree species: Chinese elm
Container length: 130 cm
Designer: Han Xuenian

On a flat, broad landscape stand more than ten
Chinese elms of good height and density. These
trees show the beauty of forests common in the
open country.

Fig. 18 *Autumn Thoughts*
Tree species: golden-edge privet (*L.ovalifolium var. aureo-marginatum*)
Type of rock: limestone
Container length: 120 cm
Designer: Li Yunlong

A forest emerges from a piece of land besieged by water. This work, which shows the allure of forests on islands, is uniquely beautiful.

2. Poetic Beauty

Though forest penjing derives its shape and layout from nature, it is by no means a mechanical imitation of a specific scene. Instead, it is a generalization or an abstraction of a natural setting, which is then artistically processed.

Generally, forest penjing consists of a primary tree and some secondary and supplementary trees. They create a striking contrast to highlight the theme of the work. The overall layout follows the inherent rule of nature: reality exists in virtuality and virtuality in reality, each promoting the other. Therefore, forest penjing can mirror the living world truthfully and vividly and expand the space for imagination.

In an excellent work of penjing, relationships of various kinds tend to be managed skillfully, including contradictory relationships such as sparsity and density, strength and gentleness, straightness and obliqueness, twistedness and uprightness, competition and cooperation, lightness and heaviness, thickness and thinness, movement and rest, skillfulness and clumsiness, growth and decay, commonness and rareness, and complexity and simplicity. The shape and layout thus created are harmonious and full of subtle change, displaying variety in unity (fig. 19).

Penjing resembles traditional Chinese landscape painting in that the two forms share similar principles of composition. Traditional Chinese landscape painting, which mirrors the aesthetic perception of Chinese art, is mainly based on natural scenery. It evolved into an independent painting style in the Sui and Tang dynasties (581–907). Though painting involves plane composition and penjing spatial composition, both forms give expression to beauty and the creator's inner emotions through the depiction of natural scenes. Natural landscapes are without feelings, but through imagination, people can project their emotions onto them and endow them with the significance of life and human meaning.

Fig. 19 *Eight Horses*
Tree species: Chinese littleleaf box
Type of rock: turtle grain stone
Container length: 180 cm
Designer: Zhao Qingquan

The work consists of a sparse forest, an open and vast grassland, tranquil water, and eight resting horses. Full of warmth, peace, romance, and tranquility, it displays poetic and picturesque beauty, featuring unity in diversity.

Fig. 20 *Autumn Thoughts*

Tree species: Chinese elm, Chinese hackberry, vitex, border privet, and trident maple
Container length: 50 cm
Designer: He Gansun

This work is based on the artistic conception created by Ma Zhiyuan (ca. 1251–post 1321), a dramatist in the Yuan dynasty (1271–1368), in his famous work, *Tian Jing Sha: Autumn Thoughts*. The work depicts a desolate scene of sunset in the suburbs in autumn and expresses the miserable state of mind of a traveler far away from home. Using five different species of tree, carefully shaped and organized, the designer fuses his own feelings with the natural energy of this work.

In creating penjing, the designer can imbue the work with his or her own ideas and emotions, transform natural scenes into displays of human affection, and manifest unlimited artistic possibilities within a limited space. The viewers are able not only to appreciate what is in the container, but also to think of the natural scenes beyond it, thus identifying themselves with those scenes. Upon the completion of a work, the designer often gives it a concise and refined name, which, sometimes, adds the finishing touch to the work, increasing its poetic and pictorial splendor and artistic beauty (fig. 20).

CHAPTER II
TECHNIQUES OF FOREST PENJING PRODUCTION

T echniques are the basis of art. To create
a fine work of forest penjing, the
relevant techniques must first be grasped,
including knowledge about types of natural
forests, forms of penjing, material selection,
and processing methods.

1. Types of Natural Forests

Natural forest landscapes are formed because
of the different hereditary characteristics
of different trees and the influence of
specific ecological settings. Different regions
and climates give rise to different forest
landscapes.

For this reason, many natural forests with
different charms have emerged, such as forests
in open country, in mountains, by water, on
islands, in swamps, in deserts, and in tropical
regions. In addition, different tree densities,
the ages of trees, and seasonal changes also
produce different forest landscapes.

In creating forest penjing, the typical
landscapes that result from a specific
ecological environment must be fully
displayed. One must therefore observe
nature in great depth, learn from nature, and
follow and utilize the laws of nature and art.

Learning from nature does not mean a
simple imitation of natural scenery. Instead,
one should make careful selections and
turn complexity into simplicity. Meanwhile,
in shaping forest penjing according to the
composition of natural forests, the artist
should integrate his or her own perceptions
into the work to achieve harmony between

On pages 24–25

Fig. 21 *Sending an Invitation to the Wind*
Tree species: Chinese littleleaf box
Type of rock: turtle grain stone
Container length: 150 cm
Designer: Yan Yongsheng

This work seems to consist of several trees, but in
fact the roots of all the trees are connected. It is a
multiple-tree forest with interconnected roots.

Fig. 22　Forests in open country: a pine forest.

Fig. 23　Forests in open country: a birch forest.

Fig. 24　Forests in open country: a eucalyptus forest.

man and nature.

Before elaborating on the making of forest
penjing, let me first introduce some of the
major types of natural forests.

Forests in Open Country: This refers
to forests on vast expanses of flat land. As a
common kind of forest, it may consist of three
or five sparsely spaced trees, a large expanse
of primitive forest, or a forest of a single tree
species. Forests in open country can also be
mingled forests consisting of two or more tree
species (figs. 22 to 24).

Fig. 25   Forests in mountains: a cypress forest.

Fig. 26   Forests in mountains: a pine forest.

Forests in Mountains: This refers to forests in mountains and hills or on highlands. The drastic topographic changes and different landscapes give rise to large expanses of primitive forests (figs. 25 and 26).

Forests by Water: This includes forests by lakes, rivers, streams, seashores, etc. These forests often go together with mountain rocks and manifest a variety of settings and tree species (figs. 27 and 28).

Forests on Islands: This refers to forests on a small piece of land surrounded by water (fig. 29).

Forests in Swamps: These forests are in swamps. Since the trees have been immersed in water for a long time, the roots are often splayed for stability (fig. 30).

Fig. 27   Forests by water: a forest by a stream.

Fig. 28   Forests by water: a forest by the seashore.

Fig. 29   A forest on an island.

Fig. 30   A forest in a swamp.

Forests in Deserts: These forests are especially tolerant of drought and barren soil (fig. 31).

Forests in Tropical Regions: Due to hot weather and abundant rainfall, the trees in these regions compete to grow upward and the speed of succession is therefore extremely rapid (fig. 32). From some roots grow buttress roots, which spread in a radial pattern. From some large branches grow flourishing aerial roots, which penetrate head-down into the soil. In this way, one tree alone constitutes a forest.

There are also other forms of natural forests, which will not be introduced here.

Fig. 31   Forests in deserts: a Euphrates poplar forest.

Fig. 32   Forests in tropical regions: a mingled forest.

2. Material Selection for Forest Penjing

The first step of making forest penjing is working out an initial plan and selecting appropriate materials. These materials mainly include plants, containers, soil, rocks, decorative ornaments, etc.

Plants

The plants used for forest penjing are mainly woody plants. They also include some grasses and mosses.

Trees with thin branches, small leaves, and high ornamental value are usually chosen for forest penjing. After some cultivation, they will resemble big trees in nature. The trees are often thin and tall, with fewer branches in the lower part of the trunk—traits that conform to the ecological features of natural forests. The trunks are either straight, oblique, or crooked. Trees with cliff-shaped trunks or trunks that are too twisted are generally not desirable.

Shallow containers are often used for

Straight Trunk: The trunk is straight and upright, largely not crooked, and the branches spread out horizontally or hang down robustly. Hierarchical in structure, they resemble ancient, towering trees in nature.

Oblique Trunk: The trunk leans to one side, slightly crooked. The main branches spread out away from the trunk. The tree looks dynamic and balanced, as elegant as an old tree in the mountains.

Crooked Trunk: The trunk winds upward like a dragon. The branches and leaves are well-spaced and in good order.

Cliff-Shaped Trunk: The trunk, which is crooked, hangs down below the mouth of the container, with branches and leaves growing upwards.

forest penjing. Therefore, the tree selected should have well-developed roots that do not grow downwards. It is better if the tree has been bred in a shallow container for some time. If the tree is used for a closeup view, its roots need to spread in all directions to give a sense of stability.

Instead of being an independent object, each of the trees in forest penjing is part of an overall scene. Therefore, the tree selected does not need to be perfect in every respect but should be able to match with other trees for harmony. Some trees, incomplete as they look, may help achieve an ideal overall effect if properly processed and organized. Normally, trees with very distinctive characteristics are not suitable for forest penjing, as they cannot coordinate with other trees.

For multiple-tree forests, trees should usually be of the same species. Sometimes, several species of tree can be used, but one of them must take the main position, supplemented by others for stylistic unity. In the same work, one of the trees must be tallest and thickest, with others acting as subsidiaries. Be careful not to choose trees of similar height and thickness, as it can be difficult to arrange them.

Most of the trees used for forest penjing are grown, cut, or air layered. Occasionally, smaller trees or tree stumps dug from mountains can be used as well.

The materials for multiple-tree forests and crouching single-trunk forests usually come from artificial breeding, while those for multiple-tree forests with roots interconnected, or for forests consisting of a single tree with multiple trunks, are either from artificial breeding, or, occasionally, from mountains.

Wherever they come from, the materials must be bred for some time and be appropriately processed. They cannot be used until they grow into their initially desired shapes.

The trees used for forest penjing can mainly be divided into two groups: conifers and miscellaneous trees.

Conifers: This usually refers to pines (figs. 33 and 34), spruce, dawn redwood,

Fig. 33   Conifers: the five-needle pine.

Fig. 34   Conifers: the golden larch.

Fig. 35   Junipers: the Chinese juniper.

Tree Name	Latin Name
Five-needle pine	*Pinus parviflora*
Huangshan pine	*Pinus taiwanensis*
Black pine	*Pinus thunbergii*
Japanese red pine	*Pinus densiflora*
Golden larch	*Pseudolarix amabilis*
Buddhist pine	*Podocarpus macrophyllus var. maki*
Chinese juniper	*Juniperus chinensis var. Sargentii*
Chinese weeping cypress	*Cupressus funebris*
Procumbent pearlwort	*Sabina procumbens*
Spruce	*Picea asperata*
Dawn redwood	*Metasequoia glyptostroboides*
Bald cypress	*Taxodium distichum*
Japanese yew	*Taxus cuspidata var. nana aurescens*

Fig. 36　Miscellaneous trees: the Chinese elm.

Fig. 37　Miscellaneous trees: the Purpus privet.

junipers (fig. 35), bald cypress and Japanese yew, all of which are ideal for making penjing. They are mostly evergreens. They look majestic and elegant or vigorous and unrestrained. The penjing made from these trees focus on expressing the inner spirit. Common tree species in this category are shown in the table on facing page.

Miscellaneous Trees: This refers to all the tree species used to make forest penjing besides conifers. They are appreciated for their posture (fig. 36), leaves (fig. 37), flowers, and fruits. Most of them are deciduous trees, either gentle and exquisite or elegant and graceful. With rich colors that change with the seasons (fig. 38), they are often used to express unique tastes. The major tree species in this category are shown in the table on the right.

Fig. 38　Miscellaneous trees: the Japanese maple.

Tree Name	Latin Name
Chinese elm	*Ulmus parvifolia*
Chinese sweet plum	*Sageretia theezans*
Japanese zelkova	*Zelkova serrata*
Chinese hackberry	*Celtis sinensis*
Chinese littleleaf box	*Buxus sinica*
Orange jasmine	*Murraya paniculata*
Polan	*Poilaniella Fragilis*
Chinese tamarisk	*Tamarix chinensis*
Hornbeam	*Carpinus turczaninowii*
Purpus Privet	*Ligustrum quihoui*
Chinese banyan	*Ficus microcarpa*
Fukien tea	*Carmona microphylla*
Chinese ash	*Fraxinus chinensis*
Japanese maple	*Acer palmatum*
Trident maple	*Acer buergerianum*
Maidenhair tree	*Ginkgo biloba*
Crape myrtle	*Lagerstroemia indica*
Azalea	*Rhododendron simsii*
Flowering quince	*Chaenomeles speciosa*
Snowrose	*Serissa japonica*
Pomegranate	*Punica granatum*
Diamond-leaf persimmon	*Diospyros rhombifolia*
Golden beans	*Fortunella venosa*
Golden marble	*Diospyros armata*
Firethorn	*Pyracantha fortuneana*
Bamboo	*Bambusoideae*

Containers

Containers are where trees that form forest penjing are planted. They are indispensable to the overall composition of forest penjing. If forest penjing were viewed as three-dimensional landscape painting, then the container is the paper on which the painting is painted.

"Containers" refers not only to common containers, but also to many substitutes, such as stone slabs, wooden boards, and rocks.

The containers for forest penjing are normally very shallow. A deep container will dwarf the trees and reduce the sense of spaciousness. Contrarily, a shallow container can make the trees appear tall and large, create a more far-reaching visual effect, and increase the spaciousness. In addition, in a shallow container, one can pile up the soil and use rocks to create an undulating terrain, imbuing the work with more rustic charm.

For a board-shaped container or a container with a very shallow mouth, no weep holes are needed. However, a deeper container must have one or two weep holes in appropriate places to drain water.

According to their textures, containers can be classified into Chinese clay pots (fig. 39), glazed pots (fig. 40), marble pots (fig. 41), naturally shaped stone pots, and specially shaped clay pots (fig. 42). There are also some containers made of concrete, which are mainly used for extra-large forest penjing (fig. 43). Generally, Chinese clay pots are good for conifers and junipers and glazed pots for miscellaneous trees. Marble pots and naturally shaped stone pots can be used for all tree species.

Containers are mostly naturally shaped, rectangular or oval. They can also be round or square. Their shape should be simple and concise. Sophisticated designs or complicated lines should be avoided. Naturally shaped stone pots and specially

Fig. 39 Chinese clay pot.

Fig. 40 Glazed pot.

Fig. 41 Marble pot.

Fig. 42 Specially shaped clay pot.

shaped clay pots are irregular in shape and richly diverse. When used for forest penjing, they can show rustic charm.

The ratio between the length and width of a container is mainly determined by the depth of field and is normally about 2:1. For greater depth of field, the ratio can be 1:1, i.e. in containers that are square or round. Rectangular or boat-shaped containers can be used for scroll-shaped works.

The color of the container must form a harmonious contrast with the trees. Based

Fig. 43   Concrete base used for an extra-large forest penjing.

on the color of the landscape, it is most often white, light gray, light green, light blue, or purplish red. Evergreen conifers and junipers are often equipped with red or purple Chinese clay pots, creating a scene of classical elegance. Miscellaneous trees, especially their foliage, and flowering and fruiting trees are rich in color. Choosing glazed pots with a brightly-colored sheen can produce a better viewing effect.

No fixed proportion is set between the length of the container and the height of the landscape. This is normally decided according to artistic preference. The width of the container can be determined by the depth of the forest.

The scroll is a unique form of Chinese painting. It extends horizontally to as long as 5 m. For example, *Scenes Along the River During the Qingming Festival*, a well-known painting by Zhang Zeduan that depicts urban life in the capital of the Northern Song dynasty (960–1127), is 24.8 cm high and 528 cm long.

Scenes Along the River During the Qingming Festival (detail)

Soil

The trees in forest penjing grow in the limited space of a container. To ensure their healthy development, they must be offered sufficient water, air, and nutrients of different kinds. The soil in the pot can store and supply water, air, and nutrients to the trees to maintain their growth. This contributes greatly to the trees' healthy development. The soil also stabilizes the trees and shapes the terrain of the forest penjing.

A good soil mix should fulfill the following requirements. It should be able to hold sufficient water to meet the growth needs of the plant, enable the plant to gradually absorb nutrients from fertilizer, ensure there is enough air for the roots by draining away extra water in a timely fashion, and satisfy the needs of the plant for soil acidity and alkalinity. It should also be free of germs, viruses, worm eggs, and chemical residues.

The soil can be organic or non-organic. Organic soil mainly refers to peat soil (fig. 44), humus soil, pine bark (fig. 45), etc. These soils have good water-holding capacity and can be sterilized by high temperatures or under the blazing sun. Non-organic soil mainly refers to mountain sand (fig. 46), volcanic soil (such as akadamatsuchi or red ball earth, and kanuma pumice or kanuma soil mostly used in Japan) (figs. 47 and 48), weathered granite, expanded clay, etc. Non-organic soil has good drainability, allowing fresh air to keep entering the soil.

When making penjing in different regions, one can use local materials to make the soil mixture oneself based on the needs of different tree species. Generally, more non-organic soil is used for conifers and more organic soil is used for miscellaneous trees.

In addition, different tree species require soil of different chemical properties. Some respond well to slightly acidic soil; others may prefer alkaline soil. Therefore, the choice should be made based on the biological property of the trees. The pH value of the soil required by most tree species is between 6 and 7.5.

Before laying the soil, coarse particles must first be sifted out with a coarse soil

Fig. 44   Peat soil.

Fig. 45   Pine bark.

Fig. 46   Mountain sand.

Fig. 47   Akadamatsuchi.

Fig. 48   Kanuma pumice.

sieve set, then the remaining soil divided into coarse-grained soil and fine-grained soil using a less coarse soil sieve set, and finally the dust removed from the fine-grained soil with a fine mesh sieve set. Since the containers for forest penjing are very shallow, the soil used should not be too coarse.

Rocks

Forests in nature, especially those in mountains, cannot possibly exist without rocks. In some cases, trees actually grow on top of rocks. Therefore, rocks are often used to supplement forest penjing, thereby displaying the beauty of nature.

Rocks are selected based on their shape, texture, and color. Rocks used for forest penjing should have natural shapes, gentle colors, and fine textures. They should not have sharp corners or overly narrow wrinkles on their surface. Rocks can be hard or cancellous. Hard rocks are often selected for their fine textures in the making of forest penjing. The following three types are the most common.

Turtle Grain Stone: This rock is hard and mostly round with wrinkles on the surface that resemble those on a turtle shell and colors that are simple and classic. It absorbs water and gathers moss. It ranges in color from yellowish gray to blackish gray to light gray. Found mainly in China's Sichuan, Anhui, Shandong, Hubei, and Guizhou provinces, this rock is ideal for forest penjing (fig. 49).

Yingde Stone: This is one of the traditional Chinese ornamental rocks. It is hard and generally rugged but occasionally perfectly round. Its wrinkles vary in degree of thickness. This rock basically does not absorb water or gather moss. It is usually grayish black or light gray and occasionally it has white veins. Yingde stone is mainly found in China's Guangdong Province (fig. 50).

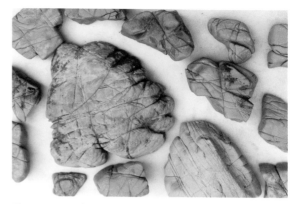

Fig. 49   Turtle grain stone.

Fig. 50   Yingde stone.

Fig. 51   Pebbles.

Pebbles: Pebbles are very hard and mostly oval-shaped. They have a smooth surface and do not absorb water or gather moss. Irregular pebbles with some surface wrinkles are often chosen for forest penjing. Pebbles are found in many places, such as mountain streams, creek mouths, waterfronts, and underwater placers (fig. 51).

Fig. 52 *Intoxicating Autumn*
Tree species: Japanese maple
Container length: 100 cm
Designer: Zhao Qingquan

This work consists of 7 Japanese maples of different sizes. It depicts a forest scene common in the open country. It is a typical multiple-tree forest penjing.

Fig. 53 Clay ornaments.

On facing page

Fig. 54 *A Scene in the Region of the Yangtze and Huaihe Rivers*
Tree species: trident maple
Type of rock: turtle grain stone
Container length: 100 cm
Designer: Liu Chuanfu

This work consists of two groups of trident maples and several pieces of turtle grain stone. The work has an undulating land base. It depicts a forest common in mountains.

Decorative Ornaments

Decorative ornaments are the miniature buildings, figures, and animals placed in forest penjing as decorations. Properly arranged, they can add to the appeal of a work of forest penjing and enhance its artistic expression. Of the various textures of ornament, clay ornaments are best, because they respond well to water or high temperatures and easily coordinate with the container and rock. The clay ornaments commonly found in forest penjing include buildings, figures, animals and boats and are produced in Shiwan of Guangdong Province (fig. 53). To personalize a work, the artist can make ornaments using natural materials such as wood, bamboo, and rocks.

3. Forms of Forest Penjing

Natural forests are diverse and rich in variety. Forest penjing falls into many types, each of which has different requirements. For better research and artistic creation, it is necessary to classify different types of forest penjing.

In practice, forest penjing can be classified based on different standards, such as forest structure, growing mode, tree type, density, and the distance between trees.

Classification Based on Forest Structure

A Multiple-Tree Forest: No less than three independent trees are planted in the same container (figs. 52 and 54).

Fig. 55 *Sunshine in Spring*

Tree species: flowering quince
Tree height: 108 cm
Designer: Zhao Qingquan

Three plants grow out of the same root in picturesque disorder. Together, they form a forest consisting of a single tree with multiple trunks.

Fig. 56 *Refined Mountain Forest*

Tree species: Chinese elm
Container length: 110 cm
Designer: Hu Chunfang

This work is a forest consisting of a single tree with multiple trunks, growing from an old stump dug out of a mountain. With good placement and density, the trees portray a forest scene found in mountains.

A Multiple-Tree Forest with Interconnected Roots: Three or more trees with interconnected roots are planted in the same container (fig. 57 and see fig. 21 on pages 24 and 25).

A Forest Consisting of a Single Tree with Multiple Trunks (figs. 55 and 56).

Fig. 57 *Towering into the Sky*

Tree species: trident maple
Tree height: 100 cm
Designer: Liu Chuanfu

This work consists of trident maple stumps dug from a mountain. The roots are from the same stump and are interconnected.

Fig. 58 *A Single Tree Forming a Forest*

Tree species: golden beans
Container length: 100 cm
Designer: Zhu Yinan

The trees are artificially bred. The main trunk lies on the ground with branches growing out of it, creating a forest. It is a typical crouching single-trunk forest.

Below

Fig. 59 *Ambition*

Tree species: Chinese hackberry
Container length: 120 cm
Designer: Wu Chengfa

This work uses Chinese hackberries dug from mountains. Branches originating from the crouching main trunk form a crouching single-trunk forest.

A Crouching Single-Trunk Forest: The branches on a crouching trunk are made into three or more trees, which form a forest. The trees are either artificially bred (fig. 58) or dug out from mountains (fig. 59).

Classification Based on Growing Mode

A Standard Forest: This is the most common form of forest penjing. The trees are directly planted in the container and, sometimes, some small rocks and ornaments are arranged beside them. This method is often used to display open country forests (fig. 60 and see fig. 5 on page 8).

A Water and Land Forest: There are two parts—land and water—in a container, usually divided by a stone slope bank. Trees are planted on the land and the rest of the space is filled with water. In some cases, the space is purposefully left dry to only give the impression of water. This type of penjing is mostly used to display waterside forests (see fig. 8 on pages 12 and 13 and fig. 127 on pages 84 and 85).

A Forest on Rocks: A rock is arranged in the container and all the trees grow on it. This is mostly used to display mountainous forests (fig. 61).

Fig. 60 *Listening to Pines*
Tree species: five-needle pine
Tree height: 60 cm
Designer: Zhao Qingquan

Several five-needle pines of different sizes are arranged in a shallow pot based on a forest penjing layout. This work depicts a standard forest.

Fig. 61 *Picking Chrysanthemums by the Eastern Fence*

Tree species: Chinese juniper
Type of rock: limestone
Container length: 150 cm
Designer: Fan Yicheng

With all of its trees growing on rocks, this work shows the landscape of a mountain forest.

Fig. 62 *Persimmons Turning Red Overnight in Autumn*

Tree species: diamond-leaf persimmon
Tree height: 85 cm
Designer: Liu Chuanfu

This work consists of three persimmon trees of varied height and density. It is a typical three tree forest penjing.

On facing page, top

Fig. 63 *Charm*

Tree species: Japanese maple
Type of rock: limestone
Container length: 80 cm
Designer: Zhao Qingquan

This work, a typical thin forest scene, consists of five Japanese maples of varied priority and density.

On facing page, bottom

Fig. 64 *Pastoral Charm*

Tree species: Chinese hackberry
Container length: 160 cm
Designer: Wu Chengfa

This work consists of two groups of Chinese hackberries with connected roots. The layout is complicated and the trees vary in height and density. It resembles a dense forest.

Classification Based on Forest Density

A Three Tree Forest: Normally, three independent trees or three trees with a shared root are planted together. This is the simplest forest landscape and the basis for forest penjing (fig. 62).

A Thin Forest: Normally, at least five to nine independent trees are planted together or five to nine plants grow out of the same root.

With a relatively complicated layout, they can be used to display sparse yet picturesque forest landscapes (fig. 63).

A Dense Forest: Many trees, or trees from the same root, are arranged together normally. This type of work has the most complicated layout of any form of forest penjing, expressing a luxuriant forest landscape (fig. 64).

Fig. 65 *Spring Charm*

Tree species: bald cypress
Container length: 150 cm
Designer: Han Xuenian

This work consists of dozens of thin bald cypresses of similar size and shape. Focusing on the overall layout and the variety present in the blank space in the middle, the work aims to depict the landscape of a distant forest.

Fig. 66 *The Sound of Wind Is Heard from Afar*

Tree species: five-needle pine
Type of rock: turtle grain stone
Container length: 180 cm
Designer: Zhao Qingquan

This water and land penjing has a big tree as the primary tree and focuses on displaying the details of the trunk, bringing to mind the landscape of a nearby forest.

Classification Based on the Distance Between Trees

A Nearby Forest: The trees are thicker and fewer in number and the distinction between the primary and secondary trees is clear. Each of the trees must vary in shape and be able to coordinate with the others (fig. 66).

   A Distant Forest: The trees are large in number but are of similar sizes and shapes. The layout emphasizes the overall outline and space (fig. 65).

Tree Penjing (Specifications Based on Tree Height)	
Extra-large	Over 120 cm
Large	90–120 cm
Medium	50–90 cm
Small	16–50 cm

Note: tree height refers to the distance between the root above ground and the tip of the tallest branch.

Water and Land Penjing (Specifications Based on Container Length)	
Extra-large	Over 120 cm
Large	90–120 cm
Medium	50–90 cm
Small	16–50 cm

Fig. 67 *A Vast Forest*
Tree species: Chinese elm
Tree height: 115 cm
Designer: Chen Jianhua

Straight, upright Chinese elms of different heights are arranged together. The primary tree is set slightly forward and the smaller trees slightly backward in order to resemble a forest viewed from near to far.

A Forest for Viewing From Near to Far:
The distinction between the primary and the secondary trees is apparent. The primary tree is often arranged in the center of the container, slightly forward, with the smaller trees in the rear, to create a visual effect of trees ranging from large to small (fig. 67).

In addition, like other types of penjing, forest penjing can also be extra-large, large, medium, small, or miniature. For precise specifications, refer to the tree penjing and water and land penjing guidelines on page 45. Due to the restrictions of the natural properties of trees, miniature forest penjing is not common.

4. Tools and Instruments

The tools and instruments mainly used to make forest penjing include:

Planting Tools (fig. 68)

Soil Sieve Set: This is used to sift out coarse particles. The mesh has multiple sizes.

Root Hook: This is used to remove old soil on the root during repotting. The tool may have one, two, or three hooks.

Flowerpot Hole Mesh Pad: This is a pad placed on the weep hole of the container.

Soil Scoop Set: This is used to move soil into the container. Some of the tools have a thin net at the bottom that can sift out dust in the soil.

Bamboo Rod: This is used to tightly press the soil against the roots.

Soil Compressor: This is used to compress soil and moss in the container.

Coco Brush: This is used to clean the container surface and the working table.

Soil sieve set

Root hook

Soil scoop set

Flowerpot hole mesh pad

Bamboo rod

Soil compressor

Coco brush

Fig. 68 Planting Tools

Shaping Tools (fig. 69)

Standard Shear: This is used to cut branches that are not too thick.

Root Shear: This is used to cut roots or relatively thick branches.

Concave Branch Cutter: This is used to cut thick side branches. The cutter can be large, midsized, or small.

Long Slim Twig Shear: This is used to trim twigs that are close to one another. The shear can be large or small.

Garden Shear: This is used to cut thick branches and roots.

Knob Cutter: This is used to remove ugly knots on branches or shorten thick roots.

Coils of Metal Wire: These are used to shape the branches through wiring. The coils can be made of aluminum or copper wire of different specifications.

Wire Cutter: This is used to cut wire. There are many different kinds of wire cutters.

Wire Pliers: These are used to wire and

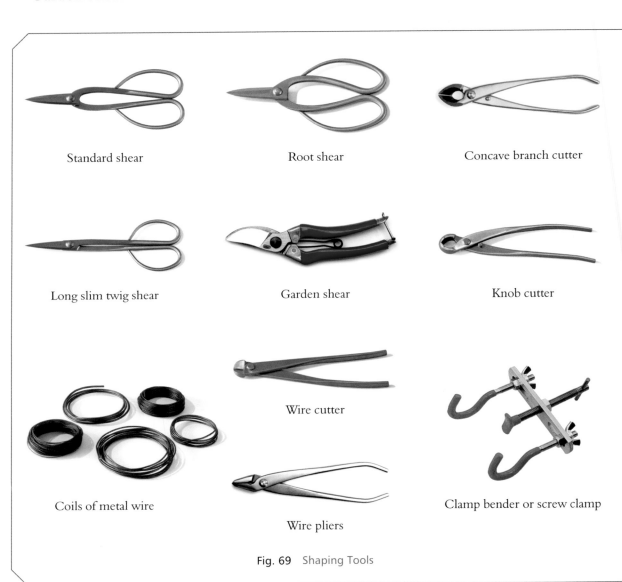

Standard shear	Root shear	Concave branch cutter
Long slim twig shear	Garden shear	Knob cutter
Coils of metal wire	Wire cutter Wire pliers	Clamp bender or screw clamp

Fig. 69 Shaping Tools

unwire the branches.

Clamp Bender or Screw Clamp: This is used to adjust relatively thick branches.

Garden Saw or Sickle Saw: This is used to cut branches and roots that are too thick.

Turntable: This is used to process penjing and includes a tabletop turntable and floor turntable.

Hammer: This is used to process rocks. The types of hammer include a ball peen hammer and a hammer with a pointed tip.

Chisel: This is used to carve and process rocks.

Maintenance Tools (fig. 70)

Watering Can: This is used to water the plants and apply liquid fertilizer.

Mist Sprayer: This is used to spray pesticide solution or mist. It can be hand-powered or any variety of electric device.

Tweezers: These are used to pick buds, remove decaying leaves and useless grasses, and catch pests.

Garden saw or sickle saw

Floor turntable

Ball peen hammer

Chisel

Watering can

Mist sprayer

Tweezers

Fig. 70 Maintenance Tools

5. Source Material Processing

After the trees and rocks are chosen, they must be processed before they are arranged.

Processing Trees

Trees, whether they are stumps dug from mountains or small trees artificially bred, normally need one to two years of breeding before they can be further shaped and assembled.

During the breeding period, it is better if the tree is planted in a shallow pot, so that it can become adapted to shallow pots when it grows bigger. During this period, the tree should also be trimmed and shaped. In addition, control of pests and diseases should also be undertaken.

When a tree is processed, it should first be carefully examined from different angles and directions to find its strengths and weaknesses. Sometimes, the soil on the surface must also be removed to make the structure and run of its roots clear. Finally, decisions must be made on the basic shape and direction of the tree, the angle of its main trunk, and the structures of roots, trunk and branches based on the characteristics of the tree and the overall design of the work. Meanwhile, one should also consider how to make best use of the strengths of the tree and bypass its weaknesses.

Both pruning and wiring should be undertaken in order to process a tree. Generally, wiring is used for conifers and junipers, and pruning for miscellaneous trees.

Wiring

By coiling metal wires around the limbs of the tree, the tree can be bent into a desired position and held in place by the wire.

To avoid breaking the branch or damaging the bark of the tree, a layer of hemp fiber or cloth can be wrapped around the branch (fig. 71).

Aluminum or copper wires are often used for wiring. Wires of different thickness can be chosen in accordance with the thickness and hardness of the trunk and branch. Wiring proceeds in this order: (1) main trunk; (2) main branch; (3) other branches. The wire can be wrapped clockwise or anticlockwise, but it cannot cross (fig. 72). When the wire is wrapped, it must cling to the trunk or branch at an angle of about 45 degrees and should not be wound too tightly or loosely. Bend the branch while twisting it. Be careful not to use too much force in case the branch breaks or the bark of the tree is damaged (fig. 73).

The metal wire wrapping around the main trunk from the root upwards must be fixed in the soil. After the first coil is fixed around the main trunk, the wire can continue to be wrapped upward until wiring is complete. The end of the wire should be twisted in

Fig. 71   Wrap a layer of hemp fiber around the branch.

Fig. 72   Wrap the metal wire around the branch.

Fig. 73   Bend the branch while twisting it.

Symmetrical branches.

Cut one of the symmetrical branches.

Parallel branches.

One of the parallel branches is usually cut.

Crossing branches.

One of the crossing branches is usually cut.

Overlapping branches.

Cut one of the overlapping branches.

Whorled branches.

Leave one of the whorled branches and cut the others.

Fig. 74 General Pruning Principles

reverse to prevent it from loosening. One wire can be used to fix two branches.

The wires are usually removed half a year to one year after being applied based on the species of the tree and its growth. Careful observation should be made during the growing season. The wire should be removed in a timely manner, before it sinks into the bark of the tree. The wire should be removed in the direction opposite to that in which it was wrapped to avoid damaging the bark. Thicker wires and wires that sink into the bark of the tree must be cut before they are removed.

Pruning

Pruning means cutting or shortening the redundant trunks and branches of the tree, so that they look vigorous, natural, and well-structured.

The general pruning principles (fig. 74) are as follows: first, cut unnecessary, diseased, and weak branches. Second, appropriately trim symmetrical branches, parallel branches, crossing branches, overlapping branches, whorled branches, etc. Finally, determine the length and density of the branches in accordance with the tree species and the overall design of the work.

1

Long branches needing to be cut.

2

Secondary branches

Primary branches

A pair of side branches after cutting, or the secondary branches.

3

Secondary branches

Wait until the secondary branches grow to an appropriate thickness.

4

Tertiary branches

Secondary branches

Cut the secondary branches again, leaving a pair of side branches, or the tertiary branches.

5

Continue this process as the branches grow.

Fig. 75 Pruning Long Branches

The long branches can be cut only when they grow to an appropriate thickness. When the secondary branches grow out, leave two of them and cut the rest. Continue this process for the tertiary and fourth branches. Generally, two branches are left at each stage, one longer and the other shorter, in the shape of a scissor. Occasionally, one or three branches can also be kept to vary the density (fig. 75).

Sometimes, some big branches need to be cut to achieve overall harmony (fig. 76). Additionally, some roots that are too long, especially thick roots that grow downwards, also need to be shortened to adapt them to a shallow pot.

Fig. 76 Cut big branches from some trees.

Processing Rocks

In forest penjing, rocks, which mostly serve as ornaments, are not much used. In water and land forest penjing, rocks appear as ornaments above ground as well as in water. They can also be used to form a slope bank. Therefore, after being processed, they are used on many occasions to achieve a better layout. Rocks can be processed using the following methods.

Cutting: Rocks used to make slope banks or as ornaments on the water surface must have their bottoms cut flat so that they lie naturally and neatly on the bottom of the container. Before cutting, the rocks should be carefully examined and the most appropriate places for cutting should be decided upon. Rocks used as ornaments above ground generally do not need to be cut. Instead, their bottoms can be buried in the soil. However, if the rocks are too big, part of them can be removed.

Cancellous rocks can be cut with a steel saw and hard rocks with a stonecutter (fig. 77). The bottoms should be cut flat and extra care should be taken to avoid damaging the rock edges.

Chiseling: This means processing a rock into its desired shape using a chisel or special pointed hammer. Chiseling is mainly used for processing cancellous rocks (fig. 78).

Polishing: This refers to the polishing of the rock surface with a grinding wheel or a piece of waterproof abrasive paper to remove its edges and corners, erase the trace of human effort, or treat damages on the rock surface. The rock can be polished first with a grinding wheel and then with abrasive paper (fig. 79).

Splicing: This means piecing together two or more rocks that have the same color and similar wrinkles, then gluing them with concrete. Most of the slope banks in water and land penjing are formed by splicing multiple rocks together (fig. 80).

Fig. 77　Cut the rock with a stonecutter.

Fig. 78　Chisel the rocks.

Fig. 79　Sand the rock down with waterproof abrasive paper.

Fig. 80　Piece the rocks together.

6. Making Forest Penjing

After the materials for forest penjing are processed, the container, trees, and other materials can be placed on the operating floor (fig. 81), the materials carefully examined, and work begun once an initial plan is made.

Composition

This refers to the arrangement of trees and other materials in the container. It is mainly used in multiple-tree forest penjing. Other types of forest penjing follow the same principles. In water and land forest penjing, the locations of rocks and the water surface also need to be considered.

In forest penjing composition, no matter how many trees are available, three of them are usually focused upon at the start: the primary tree, which is the tallest and thickest, the secondary tree, and the supplementary tree. This is the basic unit for the composition of all types of forest penjing.

In distinguishing the three trees, both height and thickness need to be considered. Ignorance of either of these qualities will result in ambiguity in priority.

First, the location of the primary tree should be determined. Viewed from the front, it should not be in the center, nor at the edge,

Fig. 82 Viewed from the front, the primary tree should not be in the center, nor at the edge, but should be arranged about one-third of the way from the left or right side of the container.

but should be arranged about one-third of the way from the left or right side of the container (fig. 82). Viewed from the side, it should be in the center of the container, slightly forward or slightly back.

After the location of the primary tree is determined, the secondary and supplementary trees can be arranged according to personal intuition. They can be arranged either in the front or in the rear, and their locations can be adjusted as needed. The secondary tree is normally arranged one-third of the way from the far side of the container (fig. 83). The

Fig. 81　Prepare the pot and trees.

Fig. 83   Arrange the secondary tree.

Fig. 84   Arrange the supplementary tree.

supplementary tree should be close to the primary tree but not parallel with it (figs. 84 to 87).

The roots of the three trees (i.e. the center of the tree trunk on the surface of the soil), if connected, must form a scalene triangle, and so must the tree canopy. This is the most fundamental layout, although it can be adjusted slightly.

The number of trees in a forest penjing is usually odd, i.e. three, five, seven, nine, etc. An even number of trees, i.e. four, six, or eight is not common, because it is not convenient for composition. However, when the number

Fig. 85   Add another supplementary tree.

Fig. 86   Continue to add supplementary trees.

Fig. 87   Add one more supplementary tree to complete the arrangement.

of trees is very large, whether this number is odd or even becomes less important.

If the composition of three trees is well understood, the same rules can be followed with a greater number of trees. For instance, if five trees are planted together, two supplementary trees can be added, one close to the primary tree and the other close to the secondary tree. If there are seven trees, two more supplementary trees should be added according to the above rule. The same rule applies to the arrangement of even more trees. In this way, the original three trees evolve into three groups of trees, but the fundamental principle remains unchanged, i.e. any of the roots of the three trees should form a scalene triangle and should not be on the same straight line; the canopy should also be scalene, with an uneven outline. If the artist has more trees prepared, better choices can be made.

The rocks in forest penjing should complement the trees and naturally match the soil. They should also vary in size and density.

In the composition of water and land penjing, the locations of the trees should be determined first, then the rocks should be arranged in a way that complements the trees well. The rocks should first be used to make slopes and banks that separate water and land, then serve as ornaments. They should be higher in a close-up view and lower in a distant view. The rocks in the middle should vary in height to create an undulating effect. Additionally, they

should also differ in size to look natural and vivid.

To improve the way forest penjing is laid out, time should be spent observing natural forests. Additionally, one can also borrow from Chinese landscape painting. The methods these paintings use to portray trees and rocks can be used in the making of forest penjing.

Tree Planting

While designing forest penjing, instead of strictly obeying the rules of tree planting, one can simply place the trees in a container. However, once the initial layout is determined, the trees need to be replanted very carefully in their container.

Before a tree is planted, its roots should first be combed carefully so that the tree fits into the container perfectly. Care should be taken that the distance between trees also meets the layout requirement.

Cover the weep hole in the container with a mesh pad, spread a layer of soil at the point where the tree is to be planted and then plant the tree there. Make sure that the originally chosen location and tree height remain unchanged. If the tree is not tall enough, add soil to make it taller. If it is too tall, shorten the descending roots.

If a flat container such as a stone slab,

Fig. 88   When a flat container is used, a fence made of special clay must be built before the plant is moved in. Metal wires must be put in place beforehand to fasten the trees.

Fig. 89   After the trees are fastened, use the soil
scoop set to cover the roots with soil. During this
process, press the soil tightly against the roots by
hand or with a bamboo rod until they are completely
buried.

Fig. 90   The trees are all planted.

wood board, or natural slate is used as the
container, a fence made of special clay must
be built before the plant is moved in so that
soil can be kept in the container (fig. 88). The
clay can be made with ordinary clay mixed
with green moss and water.

After the location of the tree is determined,
in order to stabilize it, its roots should be
fixed to the bottom of the container with
metal wires. In multiple-tree forest penjing,

this should be done with each tree.

When everything is ready, the tree can
be moved to its predetermined place in the
container. In multiple-tree forest penjing, the
primary tree should be arranged first, then
the secondary and then the supplementary
trees. After all the trees are moved into the
container, they should be carefully examined
and necessary adjustments should be made to
ensure they meet expectations.

After the trees are fastened, use the soil
scoop set to cover the roots with soil. Press
the soil tightly against the roots by hand or
with a bamboo rod until they are completely
buried (figs. 89 and 90). Then pile up soil and
use rocks to create an uneven terrain (fig. 91).

Normally, soil is piled up to form the
desired terrain. The terrain of forests in open
country is less undulating than that of forests
in mountains or along streams. The outline
of the tree should also match the terrain,
forming two flowing, wavy lines that interlace
each other.

Sometimes, ornamental rocks can be
arranged on the soil surface to help emulate
the feel of a mountain forest. They are often
partially buried in soil, as if they grew out of
it (fig. 92 on page 58).

After the container is filled with soil, the

Fig. 91   Pile up soil and use rocks to create an
uneven terrain.

soil compressor can be used to gently press the surface of the soil along the edge of the container until it is tight. When this is done, one can proceed to the next step.

So far, the planting of trees in the making of ordinary forest penjing has been introduced. Next, a few more words will be said on water and land penjing.

After the tree is basically stabilized in the container, first, glue the ornaments and the rocks for slope banks with concrete or adhesive and also fix them in the container. Then, fill the container with soil and make sure the rocks and soil surface are well matched. After that, pile up the soil and arrange the ornamental rocks to make an uneven terrain.

The rocks must be perfectly glued. They should combine well with the container, as well as with one another. They should not leak or have redundant concrete on their surface. Concrete can be removed from a rock surface with a small brush or a brush pen.

The chosen concrete should solidify fast and can be used after being mixed well with water. An appropriate amount of admixture can be added to enhance its strength. In addition, water-soluble pigment can also be added to the concrete to make its color closer to that of the rock.

Arrangement

This refers to the setup of ornaments, grasses, and mosses. Forest penjing must be able to embody some specific themes and so for better artistic effect, some ornaments can be tastefully added. Generally, the ornaments should be small in number, light in color, free in style, and proportionate in size.

The ornaments, such as houses, human figures, and animals, can be fixed onto a stone slab with waterproof adhesive before being placed in the container. A bridge is often placed across a river on both banks. Not all ornaments need to be glued onto the container; some can be arranged in appropriate places in exhibitions.

Moss is also indispensable to forest penjing. It not only integrates the trees, rocks, and soil, but also keeps the water and soil in the container, can represent grassland or bushes, and enriches the colors of the work. Since there are many kinds of mosses, in a penjing work, one kind of moss can be used principally and be supplemented by other

Fig. 92
Rocks are often buried in the soil, as if they grew out of it.

kinds, thereby achieving harmonious unity and contrast (fig. 93).

Moss usually grows in shady and humid places. It can be obtained with a small spade. Weeds should be removed before it is applied.

Before spreading moss, sprinkle a layer of fine "ornamental soil," moisten the soil surface with a mist sprayer, tear the moss into small pieces, then stick it to the surface carefully. Make sure the moss is not overlapping. The moss should not meet the rocks in a straight line, but instead should interlock naturally. Meanwhile, some small flowers or grasses can be planted to add a natural feel. When everything is done, press the moss against the soil by hand or with a soil compressor until the two are tightly combined.

After all the arrangement is complete, the trees can be carefully trimmed again (fig. 94) and everything kept well-watered with a fine-meshed watering can. Once this is done, the initial stage of a forest penjing work is finished. As it is managed in later years, it will gradually become perfect and natural.

The forest penjing just completed should

Fig. 93 Spreading moss on the surface of the soil not only integrates the trees, rocks, and soil, but also preserves water and soil. Moss can also represent grassland or bushes and enrich the colors of the work.

Fig. 94 After everything is done, carefully trim the trees again.

be placed in a windless, partly shady place and the soil must remain moist. After some time, when new roots begin to appear, it can be regularly maintained.

CHAPTER III

ARTISTIC PRINCIPLES OF FOREST PENJING

In a fine work of penjing, every item is imbued with the creator's subjective feelings, thoughts, and emotions. Like a poem that expresses rich feeling in only a few words, a forest consisting of several trees can trigger the viewer's endless imagination. A work with picturesque charm can produce a strong appeal for the viewer. It provides food for thought and is worth viewing a hundred times.

While techniques are the basis for forest penjing creation and need to be mastered, technique alone is not enough to make an excellent work of penjing. This also requires the creator to learn from nature and observe the principles of artistic composition.

In a single tree penjing, there is no consideration given to how the trees are distributed. In a penjing consisting of two trees, this is not an issue, either. However, in a forest penjing composed of three or more trees, the relationship between competition and interdependence among the trees is vital.

Fig. 96 *Gorgeous Autumn*
Tree species: diamond-leaf persimmon
Tree height: 105 cm
Designer: Liu Chuanfu

This work consists of two parts: the primary part on the left and the secondary part on the right.

On pages 60–61

Fig. 95 *An Ancient Elm Extending Out to Sea*

Tree species: Chinese elm
Type of rock: turtle grain stone
Container length: 170 cm
Designer: Zheng Yongtai

The forest growing out of the trunk of an ancient elm looks light and graceful, while the trunk, the soil, and the rocks below it are heavy and dignified. This satisfies the viewer's psychological need for balance.

Mutually transformable and with infinite variety, this relationship embodies the philosophy of unity in diversity.

The key to forest penjing composition lies in the display of overall beauty through the beauty of individual trees. Efforts should be made to exhibit not only the relationship between the roots, trunk, branches, and leaves of a single tree, but also the relationship between different trees. For this purpose, principles of composition, such as seeking unity in diversity, must be applied.

The principles are not artificial rules but are instead a summary of the beauty of composition in nature. Rather than restricting artistic creation, they help represent it. The following are some major composition principles for forest penjing.

1. Differentiating Between Primary and Secondary

This is the first and most important principle of forest penjing composition. In a work of forest penjing, there can only be one tree that is the tallest and thickest, known as the primary tree (fig. 96). All the other trees play a supplementary role. If the primary tree is not arranged in an outstanding position, the whole work will become unfocused and will lack notable features and emotional appeal.

To make the primary tree stand out, its size, angle, line, shape, and position must first be determined. Then, the other trees should be arranged in harmony with it. Finally, the trees must be furnished with rocks,

Fig. 97 *An Elegant and Beautiful View*
Tree species: Chinese ash
Type of rock: turtle grain stone
Container length: 130 cm
Designer: Zhang Zhigang

The right side of this water and land penjing is primary and the left side is secondary. On each side, there is also a sub-distinction between primary and secondary.

ornaments, and smaller plants for decoration.

It is important to clarify that the relationship between primary and secondary is relative. There is only one primary tree in the whole work; however, for each of the supplementary trees, the relationship between primary and secondary should also be appropriately managed (fig. 97).

2. Deciding on Orientation and Angle

In forest penjing, every tree, whether it is oblique or upright, should have its orientation and angle determined. The layout must not be equally balanced; instead, it should create momentum and offer vivid charm based on the orientations and angles of the trees.

First, the front of the tree, which should be the most beautiful part, must be carefully determined. Generally, viewed from the front, the trunk of the tree should not lean forward or backward. The main branches and roots visible in the air should extend outward a little on each side but be shorter at the front and back. The main branches should not be symmetrical or parallel to each other or on the same plane. If the trunk is crooked, the main branches should reach out from the bulging part instead of from the concave part.

After the front of the tree is chosen, its angle, something that has a tremendous influence on the momentum of the tree, should then be determined. An upright trunk towers straight up into the sky, an oblique one is nimble and graceful, and a crooked one looks poised for takeoff. The orientation and angle of the tree must be repeatedly adjusted to achieve the desired effect (fig. 98).

3. Density Variation

Natural scenes are varied in density. In forest penjing, if several trees are arranged evenly in a container, they are monotonous and soulless. The same trees, if arranged well according to density, resemble an expanse of natural forest. Variation in density conforms more to natural laws and can produce a better artistic effect.

All forms of art have their inner rhythms. In the composition of forest penjing, the density of trees, the lines of branches, and the roots above ground should all be dealt with appropriately to form contrast and create vitality and musical rhythm.

How to handle the issue of density is a matter of artistic judgement. It is based solely on the creator's artistic perceptions in accordance with the laws of nature (figs. 99 and 100).

Fig. 98 *Wavy Charm*
Tree species: five-needle pine
Type of rock: turtle grain stone
Container length: 60 cm
Designer: Ying Ripeng

All the trees lean in one direction. The work is kinetic and graceful.

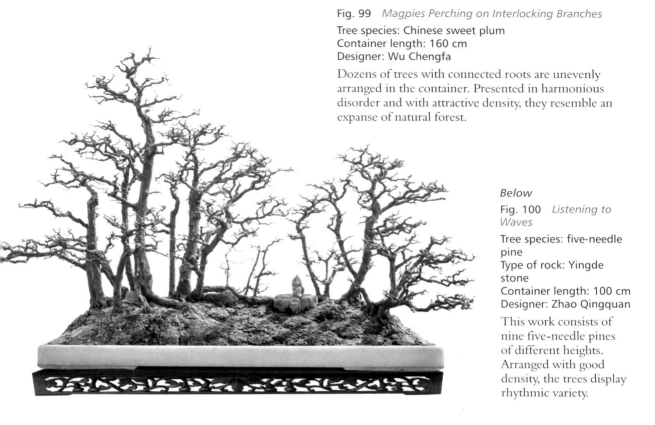

Fig. 99 *Magpies Perching on Interlocking Branches*
Tree species: Chinese sweet plum
Container length: 160 cm
Designer: Wu Chengfa

Dozens of trees with connected roots are unevenly arranged in the container. Presented in harmonious disorder and with attractive density, they resemble an expanse of natural forest.

Below

Fig. 100 *Listening to Waves*

Tree species: five-needle pine
Type of rock: Yingde stone
Container length: 100 cm
Designer: Zhao Qingquan

This work consists of nine five-needle pines of different heights. Arranged with good density, the trees display rhythmic variety.

4. Leaving Blank Space

All things in the universe reflect the unity between reality and virtuality. Reality exists in virtuality and virtuality in reality and each sustains the other. To mirror the living world truthfully and vividly, this inherent natural law must be observed.

In designing forest penjing, the relationship between reality and virtuality should be properly managed, with some blank space left where necessary. Cramming the container is taboo.

Forest penjing also embodies the art of spatial division. Spatial beauty is mainly realized through the selection of branches and leaves and the handling of density and tree placement. Too much density creates a sensation of suffocation and renders the work inflexible; too much sparsity will result in a lack of strength and meaning.

Therefore, efforts should be made to highlight what is important and add meaning to blank space (fig. 101). The whole work, straightforward but not simple, should put

Fig. 101 *High Mountains and Flowing Water*
Tree species: five-needle pine
Type of rock: limestone
Container length: 130 cm
Designer: Zhang Zhigang

Through careful spatial division, these pines look understated but not simplistic.

viewers right at the scene, making them feel as if they were on a winding path leading to a secluded place.

The relationship between virtuality and reality is relative. In terms of forest penjing as a whole, space is virtual, while scenery is real. However, as far as local structures are concerned, the space where trees are sparsely arranged is virtual and where they gather densely is real. A well-organized layout can combine virtuality and reality and enable each one to promote the other (see fig. 118 on pages 78 and 79).

No rules can quantify the application of virtuality and reality in the making of forest penjing. It all depends on the perception of the creator, who follows the laws of nature. It is exactly for this reason that the work embodies the personality of the creator.

5. Producing an Echoing Harmony

All the materials in the container are indispensable to a work of penjing. Instead of existing independently, they are internally related and must coordinate with each other. This interrelation is realized mainly through an echoing harmony between the materials, without which the designer would struggle to express his or her feelings (fig. 102).

Mutual gazing is reflected in the direction in which the materials "look," for example, the slanting direction of a tree or the direction in which the main branch extends. The primary tree in forest penjing should echo with other materials in direction. This is mainly reflected in that all the other objects should echo with the primary, instead of otherwise.

Mutual echoing includes echoing in tree species, shapes, lines, colors, density, weight, reality and virtuality, etc. For example, if the primary tree is straight and vigorous, other trees that echo it should have similar features. If the main scenery takes one color as the predominant color, other echoing scenery should also have this color. If a large blank space is left somewhere in the container, smaller blank spaces should be left in other parts of the container as well.

Fig. 102   *The Waterside Town in My Dream*
Tree species: Chinese elm
Type of rock: Yingde stone
Container length: 120 cm
Designer: Jiang Wenhua

Two groups of trees face each other across the water. The branches extend to each other as if saying hello. The same tree species and composition are repeated to create an echo effect.

6. Creating Harmonious Competition

Forest penjing fully exhibits the ecological mechanism of harmonious competition between natural tree communities. This is especially true of dense forests, in which all the trees extend their branches and leaves to the sky for sunlight, air and space to survive, while at the same time making way for branches of other trees extending towards them. Some trees in the center may tower up into the sky, while those on the edge may extend outwards. In this way, the trees harmoniously coexist.

In composing a work of forest penjing, this crossing and dodging must be managed well to ensure the branches are in good order. Even if it is a thin forest, the branches must simultaneously compete with and dodge each other to achieve natural charm and beautiful harmony (fig. 103).

Fig. 103 *The Beauty of Red by a Stream*
Tree species: hawthorn
Type of rock: Yingde stone
Container length: 100 cm
Designer: Wu Chengfa

The branches and leaves of the trees extend as they like, while also avoiding other branches and leaves that are extending towards them. They are numerous but remain in order. They complement each other and work together to bring out the beauty of harmonious coexistence in nature.

7. Tempering Hardness with Softness

All things in nature are masculine or feminine. Harmoniously integrated, they create scenery diverse in form and color. This is what tempering hardness with softness means.

Similarly, tree branches are also either bold and vigorous or tender and bent. When they are arranged in forest penjing, branches should combine these two qualities to produce a breathtaking artistic effect.

Trees can exhibit this combination of hardness and softness through their branches, which are either straight or curved, or through angle changes. Rocks, hard as they are, also have gentle contours, showing softness in hardness. A penjing work should not only focus on expressing what is masculine or feminine, but should also combine the two to create contrast and harmony (see fig. 9 on pages 14 and 15).

8. Balancing Light and Heavy

People sense forms and colors with their eyes. Influenced by their subconsciousness and life experience, they have different senses of weight for different visual objects. In appreciating penjing, the sizes, colors, physical features, and momentum of different scenes produce different senses of weight in people's minds.

To enable people to achieve psychological balance in penjing appreciation, one must try to achieve balance between light and heavy (see fig. 95 on pages 60 and 61).

Forest penjing adopts asymmetrical balance. Normally, the primary scenery is not in the center, but slightly to one side. At the same time, it should not be too close to the edge of the container. The scene can be heavy in the lower part and light in the upper part, not vice versa. If objects on one side of the container are concentrated and heavy, those on the other side must be scattered and light. If the trees

on one side have short branches and dense leaves, those on the other side should have long branches and sparse leaves.

In addition, rocks or ornaments are often arranged in blank space to achieve overall balance.

9. Being Both Bold and Refined

In forest penjing, trees can be thick or thin, the processing bold or refined, and the artistic style coarse or exquisite (fig. 104). In the composition of forest penjing, the big picture should first and foremost be kept in sight. Focus should first be placed on attempting to bring out the momentum and charm of the whole work, not the details. After the overall structure of the work is determined, improving the details can then be concentrated upon.

Works with different styles have different focuses. However, a bold and unconstrained work should not lack refinement and a refined work should always contain elements of

Fig. 104 *The Woodcutter Returns*
Tree species: Chinese elm
Type of rock: turtle grain stone
Container length: 120 cm
Designer: Zhao Qingquan

The tall, thick trees contrast with the slim trees beside and behind them, displaying rustic charm and creating a sense of momentum in the work.

boldness and straightforwardness. An excellent work should be both bold and refined. It should also be focused, producing momentum in contrast and unity in form and spirit.

In making forest penjing, operating at close range from beginning to end should be avoided. Instead, one should often move back and distance oneself from the work in order to form a full picture of it.

10. Balancing Between Concealing and Revealing

Art is valued for its implicitness. In the composition of forest penjing, if everything is revealed, the space for imagination is lost and the content the work intends to display is limited.

To display the depth and width of a forest, simply increasing the number of trees cannot be depended upon, as it sometimes may not work. Instead, the trees should be arranged in picturesque disorder, balanced between concealing and revealing. The trunks, branches, and leaves should interweave, some concealed and others revealed. The ornamental rocks should be partly hidden and partly visible. The rocks may hide behind the trees, or the trees behind the rocks, creating a scene that is always new.

Only when concealing and revealing are well-balanced can a vivid landscape featuring scenery within scenery be created and the work, with fewer and smaller trees than a natural forest, produce the same far-reaching effect, exciting the viewer's rich imagination (see fig. 116 on pages 76 and 77).

In addition, in the composition of forest penjing, many other relationships, sometimes contradictory, should be managed well to achieve a harmoniously diversified artistic effect, such as movement and rest, artfulness and clumsiness, flourishing and withering, or commonness and rarity.

11. Improving the Creator's Comprehensive Quality

Previously, the topic of how to follow the principles of artistic composition was discussed. However, all principles are abstract and vary from person to person in practice.

Penjing is essentially a comprehensive art, closely related to poetry, literature, painting, sculpture, calligraphy, music, dance, photography (fig. 105), and gardening (fig. 106). Therefore, ultimately, improving the creator's comprehensive quality is important to penjing creation. In a sense, the artistic standard of penjing creation hinges upon the comprehensive quality of the creator.

Fig. 105　Through the camera lens, this natural forest looks like a large forest penjing.

Fig. 106　The artistic expression of forest penjing is also adopted in gardening.

"Improving the creator's comprehensive quality" does not mean that the creator should learn everything. However, he or she should have an eye for different categories of art. Learning from Chinese painting is one of the most important ways to enhance the creator's comprehensive quality. As is often said, penjing should possess poetic and pictorial splendor. This means that to make his or her work poetic, the creator must have a profound understanding of Chinese poetry and painting.

For various reasons, the theory of penjing creation is not yet complete. However, Chinese landscape painting has advanced significantly in both theory and practice. Therefore, one should carefully observe exceptional paintings from different dynasties, learn more about painting theory, and borrow from achievements in the Chinese painting arts. Chinese painting boasts distinctive national aesthetic standards and methods of expression. Its practice of leaving blank spaces and depicting lines and natural and rustic charm is particularly meaningful to the creation of penjing, an art with unique Chinese national characteristics.

Fig. 107 *Pavilions on Celestial Mountains* (detail)
Qiu Ying (ca. 1501–ca. 1551, Ming dynasty)
Ink and color on silk
Height 118 cm × width 41.5 cm
The seven pines in the scene vary in height and are arranged with good density. Spaces of different sizes are left between the trees, bringing vitality to the whole scene. This work, in the Palace Museum in Taibei, is of high referential value to the composition of forest penjing.

Leaving Blank Space

Chinese painting theory particularly emphasizes the treatment of the relationship between virtuality and reality, which is known as *liu bai*, or leaving blank space. This technique can inject vigor into the work and offer viewers endless space for imagination. Like the pauses in music, virtuality is sometimes more powerful than reality.

If one was to view forest penjing as three-dimensional painting, a lot of blank space could be observed. The spatial beauty of penjing lies precisely in its blank space. It is achieved through the composition of scenes and treatment of density and spacing (fig. 107).

Fig. 108 *Autumn Charm*

Tree species: diamond-leaf persimmon
Tree height: 100 cm
Designer: Lu Zengqiang

The branches of the trees, varied and rhythmic, lend poetic and pictorial splendor to the whole work.

Fig. 109 *Pines on Hills* (detail)

Tang Yin (1470–1523, Ming dynasty)
Ink on paper
Height 26.5 cm × width 94.5 cm

The lines of the trees are richly varied, highly rhythmic, and magnificent.

Lines

Lines are the most unique feature in traditional Chinese art. Chinese people like to condense their feelings into different lines. Composition based on lines is a major aesthetic characteristic of Chinese painting because each line is unique. Some lines are thick, others are thin; some are bold, others are gentle; some are light, others are heavy; some rise, others fall (fig. 109). These lines are not just lines; they not only shape a work and create rhythm, force, and momentum, but also express the inner world of the creator.

If forest penjing can be viewed as three-dimensional painting, this painting technique can be applied to enhance the pictorial splendor of the work (fig. 108).

Natural and Rustic Charm

Chinese landscape painting is based on the painter's in-depth observation of nature and his or her adherence to natural laws, both of which account for the genre's wealth of natural and rustic charm. Those who often "read" Chinese landscape painting will be unconsciously influenced. With an enhanced understanding of nature and natural beauty, they can better express themselves in penjing creation.

Many concepts in Chinese landscape painting, such as forms of composition, ways to paint trees, mountains, or rocks, and the cavalier perspective (fig. 110 and see figs. 111 to 114 on pages 74 and 75), can be adopted in penjing creation (see fig. 115 on page 75).

Fig. 110 *Ma Tai Painting Treasure* (I)

Ma Tai (1886–1937) was a contemporary Chinese painter. *Ma Tai Painting Treasure* is a popular picture copybook that introduces the painting of various themes. It provides inspiration for drawing Buddhas, flowers, grasses, insects, and landscapes. In the landscape portion, it introduces ways to paint various trees, branches, and leaves. It is a must-read for students of Chinese painting. In this painting, the trees are diverse in height, full of variety, and possess good density, creating a scene filled with rustic charm. This work can be referred to when constructing miscellaneous tree forest penjing.

Fig. 111 *Ma Tai Painting Treasure* (II)

Distributed in twos and threes, the pines in the scene are common in Chinese landscape paintings. This work can serve as a good reference for pine forest penjing.

Fig. 112 *Ma Tai Painting Treasure* (III)

The trees in the painting grow by water in picturesque disorder. Some are straight and some are oblique, conforming to the law of nature. This work can be referred to in the making of water and land penjing.

Fig. 113 *Ma Tai Painting Treasure* (IV)

The trees nearby are tall and those in the distance are short. Between them are trees that serve as a transition. This piece is of reference value to works of forest penjing that present a change of view from near to far.

Fig. 114 *Ma Tai Painting Treasure* (V)

This painting depicts a bamboo grove along a stream. It can be referred to when making bamboo forest penjing.

Fig. 115 *Hermits in a Bamboo Grove*

Tree species: fernleaf hedge bamboo
Type of rock: turtle grain stone
Container length: 100 cm
Designer: Zhao Qingquan

This work, which consists of bamboo and rocks, borrows from the layout of Chinese landscape painting.

CHAPTER IV
CARE AND MAINTENANCE OF FOREST PENJING

F orest penjing is maintained and managed in the same way as ordinary tree penjing. This chapter will focus on introducing some key points in this respect.

1. Placement

Ordinarily, forest penjing should be placed outdoors in a place with good sunlight and ventilation. Especially during the growing season, a work cannot be placed indoors without sunlight or outdoors under the shade of a tree for long. Otherwise, the plants will grow poorly (fig. 117).

Since the container of a work of forest penjing is very shallow, sometimes just a piece of flat board, it does not hold much soil. Therefore, it must be appropriately covered from the sun in summer in case it is burnt. In winter, it is better to move it inside a house with good exposure to sunlight in order to stop it from freezing.

Different species of trees have different requirements for sunlight and temperature. They should be arranged in different places according to their habits and the climates in their places of origin.

Fig. 117 Normally, forest penjing should be placed outdoors with good sunlight and ventilation.

Shade-intolerant trees such as pines should be arranged in places with sufficient sunlight. Shade-tolerant plants such as the azalea, snowrose, and Chinese littleleaf box can be arranged in places with a mild temperature. Cold-tolerant trees can be placed outdoors in winter, and cold-intolerant ones must be moved into a house with an ordinary temperature or into a greenhouse.

On pages 76–77

Fig. 116 *A Spring Morning in a Plum Forest*

Tree species: Chinese sweet plum
Container length: 180 cm
Designer: Yang Jihe

This crouching single-trunk forest penjing consists of a dozen trees growing out of a trunk. They are simultaneously visible and invisible, giving the viewer the impression that there are scenes beyond scenes.

Fig. 118 *Mist and Ripples*

Tree species: Purpus privet and pomegranate
Type of rock: turtle grain stone
Container length: 100 cm
Designer: Zhao Qingquan

The scenery is real and the space is virtual. The rocks are real and the water is virtual. The trees are real in contrast with the water but they are virtual when compared with the rocks. Arranged together, they each improve one another.

2. Watering

Watering is the most routine work in penjing care and maintenance. With a shallow container and not much soil, forest penjing are particularly in need of water. However, the work must not be overwatered or the branches will grow too fast and the leaves too large. Too much water may also result in oxygen deficiency of the root due to lack of air, which will eventually cause the tree to grow poorly.

The basic watering principle is "to not water the trees until they are dry and to water them thoroughly at the right time." However, it is not easy to judge when it is appropriate to water the plants and how thoroughly they should be watered. In fact, this must be determined by many factors, such as tree species, seasons, weather, containers, and soil. Specifically, different species of trees have different habits and watering needs. Plants need to be watered differently in different growing seasons. Plants should also be watered differently depending on whether it is a sunny or cloudy day or if it is summer or winter. In addition, the size and depth of the container and the water permeability of the soil should also determine the way the plants are watered.

The container of a work of forest penjing is often wider at the mouth. Therefore, make sure to water every part of the container well.

To avoid soil being washed away, it is better to use a watering can or a fine-eyed nozzle to water the plants (fig. 119). When the weather is dry, a mist sprayer can be used to spray mist on the container, as well as on the rocks, to make the moss grow well.

3. Fertilizing

The small amount of soil in the container means that soil alone cannot provide enough

Fig. 119   Water the plants with a fine-eyed nozzle.

nutrients to the trees. For their healthy growth, they should be fertilized at the right time. However, they must not be over-fertilized, which can cause fertilizer burn.

Choice of fertilizer is determined by the characteristics and growth of the tree. Foliage plants need more nitrogenous fertilizer and flowering and fruiting plants more phosphatic fertilizer. Potash fertilizer is more often used to promote the growth of stems,

Fig. 120   Organic compound fertilizer.

Fig. 121   Box the organic compound fertilizer and place the boxes on the surface of the soil.

branches, and roots.

Normally, diluted organic fertilizer is sprayed on the surface of the soil. Organic compound fertilizer can also be put into fertilizer boxes and placed in the container (figs. 120 and 121), so that the nutrients can permeate the soil with water.

When soybean cakes and rapeseed cakes are used as fertilizer, they must first be soaked; they can only be used when diluted with water. Make sure that the fertilizer solution is not too strong, or it will damage the root.

When trees are growing too well, excess or overly strong fertilizer may cause them to overgrow, which will affect the tree shape. When they are growing poorly, they cannot endure over-fertilization. Therefore, in both cases, fertilizer should be appropriately applied. It is not advisable to fertilize trees that have undeveloped roots and have recently been moved into the container. Fertilizer should not be applied during the rest period of the trees, the early stage of the flowering and fruiting period, in hot weather, or when the soil is too wet.

4. Pruning

After a work of forest penjing is complete, the trees keep growing. Some of the fast-growing species of miscellaneous trees, if not controlled, will grow rampantly, which not only impairs the overall composition of the work, but also prevents ventilation and sunlight. This inhibits the healthy growth of the trees. Therefore, they must be trimmed for maintenance and good shape. Different from composition-oriented trimming, maintenance-oriented trimming consists of branch pruning, apical pinching, bud pinching, and leaf pruning. In addition, during the rest period each year, the trees should undergo full-scale trimming according

Fig. 122   Trim new branches that are too dense.

to the composition requirements.

Branch Pruning: Some of the miscellaneous trees grow new branches every year. Some branches are too long and some are useless. Therefore, to maintain the shape of the trees, the branches must be pruned on a regular basis, a process which mainly consists of thinning and shortening the branches (fig. 122).

Apical Pinching: To inhibit the growth of the main branches and strong branches (branches with a strong growth tendency or thick branches), and promote the balanced development of all branches, apical pinching (the removal of the tender tips of the main branches and strong branches) should take place during the growing season.

Bud Pinching: Some miscellaneous trees may grow buds on the roots or branches. These must be picked to prevent the growth of redundant branches, which mar the shape of the tree.

Leaf Pruning: The best display season for foliage trees is when they begin to show new leaves. Picking leaves allows the trees to grow new leaves twice or three times a year, extending the display season and allowing sunlight and wind to pass through. However, leaves must not be pruned too often and

Fig. 123　Remove the buds of the pines.

fertilizer must be applied at the same time. Otherwise, tree growth may be affected.

Some flowering or fruiting tree species can have some of their flowers and fruits removed if they are too numerous or too densely grown, which will add to the ornamental value of the trees.

One half to two-thirds of the length of new buds on pines should be picked before the buds grow into needles. This will create a better viewing effect (fig. 123). Cypresses should have their scale leaves picked regularly during the growing season.

5. Shaping

As its trees grow, a work of forest penjing may change in shape, improving or worsening. When this happens, maintenance-based trimming is not enough; appropriate wiring becomes necessary.

When the direction of a branch needs adjustment, especially when an upturned branch needs to be pressed down, a metal wire should be used to draw the branch towards the trunk in the desired direction (fig. 124).

6. Repotting

The soil in a work of forest penjing may become less nutritious as the trees grow and fibrous roots may increase in number. As a result, the soil may harden, affecting the air and moisture permeability and the absorption of nutrients. This is the time for repotting.

For most trees, the soil is generally replaced every three to four years. The soil of some flowering or fruiting trees should be replaced every one to two years. The replacement is often done during the rest period of the trees, preferably in spring before the trees bud.

When replacing the soil, one should carefully pull the roots of the tree out from the container, remove half to two-thirds of the old soil with a root hook (fig. 125), cut roots that are too long, remove fibrous roots that are too densely grown, place the tree back in its original place in the container, and cover the roots with new soil using the soil scoop set. During this process, the soil should

Fig. 124　Press upturned branches down with metal wires.

Fig. 125　Pull the tree out from the container and remove part of the old soil with a root hook.

Fig. 126　Apply pesticide to the plants with a mist sprayer.

be pressed tightly against the roots with a bamboo rod until they are completely buried. Each of the above steps should be followed correctly. If the original container is too small, a bigger one can be used when the soil is replaced.

For a multiple-tree forest, if the roots of the trees are connected with each other, they do not need to be separated during repotting, but the old soil should be removed and so should parts of the roots.

For water and land forest penjing, one should remove the ornamental rocks and mark their original positions before replacing the soil. Only after this is done should one pull out the trees, cut part of the roots, and replace the old soil with the new. After that, the rocks should be replaced and the moss spread out.

7. Pests and Diseases

For forest penjing, prevention and treatment for pest attacks and diseases is the same as that for other types of penjing. The difference lies in that, for forest penjing, priority should be given to prevention because, with a shallow container and less soil, they are relatively vulnerable to plant diseases and pests. Ultimately, the best way to prevent pests and diseases is to make the trees strong and vigorous.

Normally, plant diseases occur in roots, branches, and leaves. In addition to prevention with pesticides, attention should also be paid to the place where the work is arranged, the way the work is watered, and soil sterilization.

Common pests include aphids, scale insects, spider mites, lace bugs, and longhorn beetles. They should be prevented or treated with different methods—hand brushing and pesticide spraying, for example (fig. 126). In addition, the natural enemies of the pests should be protected and fallen leaves and weeds under the trees should be removed.

Plant diseases and pests vary in different regions and for different trees. Therefore, prevention and treatment can be carried out according to the protection requirements of each individual plant.

CHAPTER V
WORKS OF FOREST PENJING

The techniques described in the previous chapters are the most fundamental methods and principles of forest penjing. In the actual creation of forest penjing, however, one often encounters different situations that require the flexible application of these techniques depending on the theme and the materials available. In the following, for the reader's reference, the creation process of six different works of forest penjing composed of different tree species will be introduced.

Fig. 128 Materials obtained through air-layering propagation leading up to 2004.

Fig. 129 In the winter of 2005, the materials were chosen and trimmed.

On pages 84–85

Fig. 127 *Summer Forest*

Tree species: snowrose
Type of rock: turtle grain stone
Container length: 100 cm
Designer: Zhao Qingquan

This is a water and land forest that shows the charm of a forest by water. It is in the collection of the Montreal Botanical Garden in Canada.

1. *Sunlight Slanting Through a Thin Forest*

Tree species: Japanese maple
Height: 100 cm
Designer: Zhou Qijin

The Japanese maple is elegant and graceful. It is highly ornamental, especially in autumn when the leaves turn a dazzling red. This work is a multiple-tree forest, consisting of several Japanese maples obtained through air-layering propagation (fig. 128) (to learn about air-layering, please refer to the next work, *Spring Running Wild* on page 90). Having been bred for some time, these maples mostly have upright trunks, though some of their trunks are slightly crooked. Instead of being wired, they were all trimmed to achieve natural qualities in the breeding process.

Thirteen maples were chosen in the winter of 2005. The source trees must conform to the ecological features of natural forests and be well-suited for composition and layout. Specifically, the trees should be uniform *and* varied in style. They should have well-developed roots, but no thick roots should grow downward. The trunks should be thin and tall, with few branches in the lower parts. The branches should vary in ranking, height, and size.

Each of the selected trees were pruned and shaped (fig. 129). After that, they were

Fig. 130 Arrange the plants based on the layout requirements of forest penjing.

Fig. 131　In the autumn of 2006, the plants became more luxuriant.

Fig. 132　Viewed from the front, the canopy formed a scalene triangle.

organized based on the requirements for the composition of forest penjing: viewed from the front, the primary tree should not be in the center of the container, nor at the edge, but should be arranged about one-third of the way from the right side. If viewed from the side, it should be located in the center of the container, slightly forward. The secondary tree should be arranged about one-third of the way from the other side of the container.

All the supplementary trees should be close to the primary or secondary trees. None of the three trees in the container should be on the same straight line; instead, they should form a scalene triangle when connected (fig. 130).

In the autumn of 2006, after a whole year's breeding, the trees became more luxuriant. It was time for a full-scale repruning. After that, if viewed from the front, the tree canopy also formed a scalene triangle (figs. 131 and 132).

Fig. 133　In the spring of 2007, new leaves grew out.

Fig. 134　The branches began to resemble a buckhorn.

Fig. 135　In the spring of 2009, new leaves grew into a dense shade.

Fig. 136　What the trees looked like before the leaves fell in the early winter of 2010.

Care and Maintenance

Normally, Japanese maples should be arranged in warm and humid places with good ventilation and sunlight. In summer, when there is sufficient sunlight, they should be adequately covered from the sun in case their leaves get scorched. In winter, they should be moved indoors.

The soil in the container should be kept moist. In summer, the trees should be watered every morning and evening to prevent drastic changes in the temperature of the soil. During the growing period, they should be fertilized on a regular basis. The soil in the container should be replaced every two to three years in spring when the trees begin to bud.

When a bud appears for the first time, remove the forefront part. When the new shoot grows to four to five internodes, leave the first one or two and cut the rest. To improve the appearance of the red leaves, remove all the leaves of the maple tree before autumn begins and apply diluted liquid fertilizer to the tree once. The new leaves that grow back half a month later are gorgeously red and also fall later than usual. Trim the tree during the rest period every year.

The pests that damage the Japanese maple are mainly scale insects, slug moths, bagmoths, and longhorn beetles. The diseases are mainly powdery mildew, etc.

The trees were cultivated continuously and trimmed during the rest period every year. The branches that were too long or too dense were shortened and thinned out respectively, gradually forming a buckhorn shape. As time passed, the trees grew more and more mature (see figs. 133 to 136 on page 87 and fig. 137).

By 2012, the whole work was basically complete (figs. 138 and 139).

Fig. 137   What the trees looked like before they budded in the early spring of 2012.

Fig. 138   What *Sunlight Slanting Through a Thin Forest* looked like when it was initially completed in 2012.

Fig. 139   What the trees looked like when they budded in the spring of 2013.

2. *Spring Running Wild*

Tree species: flowering quince
Container length: 120 cm
Designer: Zhao Qingquan

The flowering quince is strong and vigorous, combining hardness and softness. In early spring, it comes into leaf before blooming, and the flowers are gorgeously red. It is highly ornamental even in autumn when the fruits become ripe. Normally, a single flowering quince is used in penjing works but more than one tree can also be used for forest penjing.

Spring Running Wild is a forest penjing consisting of a single crouching flowering quince bred via two-time air-layering propagation.

The first air-layering was done to acquire the materials for the work. In March 2002, a potted flowering quince was chosen as the mother tree. Then, a 1 to 2 cm-wide section from the lower part of a strong two-year branch was girdled, damp moss and compost were applied to the wound, and it was wrapped with plastic foil. The plastic below was tied tightly and a hole was left above for ventilation and watering. Several months later, after seeing roots grow through the moss and become well-developed, the branch was cut from the mother tree and the new plant was potted. This is how the materials for this forest penjing were obtained (fig. 140).

Fig. 140 The first air-layering in early 2002.

Fig. 141 The second air-layering in early 2004.

The second air-layering was done to make the new plant into a crouching forest. In early 2004, the new plant was fully grown. Its trunk was wired into a serpentine bend and all its big branches were made to point in the same direction and remain basically perpendicular to the trunk. After that, three different sections on the trunk were girdled, which helped the roots grow out of the cuts (fig. 141).

When roots grew out of the selected nodes, the plastic foil used for air-layering was removed, and the tree was planted in a crouching position in an appropriately sized container. The trunk was buried in soil, with all the big branches facing upward, forming a crouching single-trunk forest.

In forest penjing, the number of trees used is normally odd—that number is thirteen in *Spring Running Wild*. The primary tree is placed slightly in front, about two-fifths from the right side of the container. The crooked crouching trunk made the plants appear proportionally disordered. Meanwhile, blank spaces were also left for expressiveness and ventilation.

By 2007, branches had grown on all the trunks. The soil was replaced in winter and the crouching trunk was half revealed in air (fig. 142). After the leaves fell, the trees underwent full-scale trimming. The trunks and branches were wired for spatial adjustment (fig. 143).

In later years, the trees were pruned and shaped every year and the work gradually

Fig. 142   In the winter of 2007, the soil was replaced and the crouching trunk was revealed in air.

Fig. 143   The plants underwent full-scale trimming. The spatial relationship between the trunk and branches was adjusted using metal wires.

Fig. 144   Flowering period in the spring of 2016.

became complete. In the early spring of 2016, the work was moved into a 120 cm-long glazed container and more of the crouching trunk was revealed in air (fig. 144).

By 2018, the branches, along with the work as a whole, were well-developed (fig. 145 and see fig. 146 on page 92).

Fig. 145   In 2018, the branches gradually grew and *Spring Running Wild* was basically completed.

Care and Maintenance

The flowering quince should be arranged in a place with sufficient sunlight and good ventilation. In hot summer, it should be adequately covered from the sun. It is cold-resistant.

The soil in the container should be kept moist. Water the plant regularly during the flowering period. Take care not to allow the leaves to be scorched or dehydrated in summer. Apply fertilizer regularly during the growing season and replace the soil every three years, after autumn ends or in spring after the flowers bloom.

Cut the long branches each year after the flowers blossom to help the branches ramify. Prune the tree after the leaves fall.

The pests that damage the flowering quince are mainly aphids, slug moths, and spider mites. The most prevalent disease is rust disease.

Fig. 146　What *Spring Running Wild* looked like in the spring of 2020 when its flowers bloomed.

3. *Autumn Colors*

Tree species: Japanese maple
Tree height: 90 cm
Designer: Zhao Qingquan

This is a common forest penjing consisting of a single tree with multiple trunks. The material was obtained in 2005 from another Japanese maple through air-layering propagation at a point with a whorl of branches. After being bred in a cultivation container for two years, the overall composition of the work was basically fully formed, including the priorities, height, and spacing. In late autumn of 2007, after the leaves fell, the branches were cut and the trees were moved into a container (fig. 147).

Later, as the tree grew and gradually became more luxuriant, slight adjustments were made to the branches every year to make them more striking. Meanwhile, the tree was

Fig. 147 In the late autumn of 2007, after the leaves fell, the branches were cut and the plants were moved into a pot.

trimmed and shaped every year after it shed its leaves; the soil was replaced every two to three years (figs. 148 to 150).

Fig. 148 What the trees looked like in the early autumn of 2008.

Fig. 149 What the trees looked like in the late autumn of 2009.

Fig. 150 The soil was replaced in the early spring of 2011.

Fig. 151   What the trees looked like in the late autumn of 2012.

By 2012, the branches and leaves had become fully grown but the tree had still not reached its desired shape. Then, the branches in the lower part were drastically pruned and blank spaces were left. Meanwhile, the angles of the branches were also appropriately adjusted (figs. 151 to 153).

A forest consisting of a single tree with multiple trunks is different from a multiple-tree forest. A multiple-tree forest can have some of its trees replaced in the composition process, while the composition of a forest made up of a single tree with multiple trunks is basically determined in the initial stage of choosing materials and branches.

Fig. 152 The plants were trimmed and shaped continuously in 2014.

Fig. 153 Making a flat cut to help the tree recover.

Fig. 154   What the plant looked like in late autumn of 2015.

Fig. 155   What the plant looked like when new leaves appeared in the spring of 2018.

In this work, the tallest and thickest trunk is the primary tree and all the other trunks are supplementary trees. The trunks are straight, oblique, or acceptably crooked but are unified in style. The primary and supplementary trees can clearly be told apart. They vary in height and echo one another. The tree canopy forms an undulating pattern. All the trunks coordinate and are richly varied (figs. 154 to 156).

In a forest penjing consisting of a single tree with multiple trunks, each trunk looks like an independent tree, but is actually part of the same tree, and all of the trunks are interrelated. Therefore, in the cultivation process, the growth of each trunk can be adjusted through trimming, so that they vary in height, thickness, and density while also conforming to the requirements of composition. This is an important technique for the breeding of this type of forest penjing. For the care and maintenance of the Japanese maple, please refer to *Sunlight Slanting Through a Thin Forest*.

On facing page
Fig. 156   What the plant looked like in late autumn of 2018.

4. *Spring Blossoms and Autumn Fruits*

Tree species: pomegranate
Tree height: 90 cm
Designer: Zhao Qingquan

Some of the stumps or small trees used in forest penjing are dug from mountains but more are obtained through artificial breeding methods such as sowing, cutting, and layering. The materials for multiple-tree forest penjing are mainly acquired via artificial breeding methods like these. Cutting and layering should be done on the same mother tree.

All the trees in this work came from a potted double-trunk pomegranate tree. Branches were cut from it, which were made into new trees through cutting propagation, which were then in turn bred and assembled.

Pomegranate flowers are beautiful, and so are their fruits. When the flowers bloom, they form a delightful contrast with the tree's green leaves. In autumn, the fruits are either red or yellow. The pomegranate tree in this work has small leaves, flowers, and fruits, and is ideally proportioned for forest penjing (fig. 157).

In 2010, another double-trunk tree was obtained from the branch on the mother tree through cutting propagation (fig. 158).

By 2014, the two trees had basically taken shape. However, another small tree was needed to create a distant view, which was also obtained through cutting propagation (figs. 159 and 160).

In spring 2016, a specially shaped clay pot was chosen for this three-part work. On the right side was the primary tree (the mother

Fig. 157   The initial pomegranate tree with small leaves, flowers, and fruits.

Fig. 158   Another small tree was acquired in 2010 through cutting propagation.

tree), on the left was the supplementary tree, and in the rear was a small tree that represented a distant view. Below, the bigger trees were arranged with some azaleas for rustic charm. The multiple-tree forest penjing had basically been completed. It varied in height and had good density (figs. 161 and 162 and see fig. 163 on page 100).

Fig. 159   By 2014, the two trees had basically taken shape.

Fig. 160   One more small tree was acquired through cutting propagation.

Fig. 161   By the spring of 2016, the trees had been put together.

Fig. 162   What *Spring Blossoms and Autumn Fruits* looked like in the winter of 2018.

Fig. 163   What *Spring Blossoms and Autumn Fruits* looked like when the flowers bloomed in early summer of 2020.

From the whole creation process, one can see that each of the trees is not independent scenery, but part of an organic whole. No part can be complete individually but each coordinates with others well. Some materials, though seemingly "broken," can achieve a desirable overall effect if carefully assembled and processed.

Care and Maintenance

Pomegranate trees prefer sunlight and are drought tolerant. They should be placed in warm places with sufficient sunlight and good ventilation for the entirety of the growing season.

Ordinarily, the soil in the container should be kept moist. Summer is the growing season and the flowering season. During this period, fertilizer should be applied regularly and the soil must be sufficiently moist. Phosphatic fertilizer, especially, should be used to encourage the tree to flower and bear fruit. The soil in the container should be replaced every two to three years before the tree buds in spring or after the leaves fall in autumn. Trimming should be done during the rest period every year.

The pests that damage the pomegranate tree are mainly aphids, spider mites, scale insects, and longhorn beetles.

5. *Dancing Mountain Forest*

Tree species: trident maple
Container length: 125 cm
Designer: Zhang Zhigang

The trident maple is elegant and graceful. The leaves are beautifully shaped; they are delicate and green in spring and orange-red in autumn, with high ornamental value.

This work is a crouching single-trunk forest. The material, which was dug from a mountain, is a twin-trunk tree with clear, defined features and varied heights.

The work has gone through two stages of creation. During the first creation, the trees looked highly dynamic and were full of rustic charm, but overall, the left side was too heavy and the right side resembled bushes. In addition, the outline was flat (fig. 164).

The adjustment started in 2005. The branches were pruned to break the flat and monotonous composition and to maintain the wavy, smooth outline of the trees. As time passed, the branches gradually became well-aligned and vigorous (fig. 165).

After several years of cultivation and trimming, by the spring of 2011, the overall structure of the tree was complete (fig. 166).

Fig. 164   The original tree in the spring of 2005.

Fig. 165   All the branches were reorganized after 2005.

Then the breeding continued so that the smaller branches could develop.

In the spring of 2012, some roots that grew above ground were cut to make the roots better connected overall. Except for the branches at the top that needed to be strengthened, all of the other branches were basically ready (fig. 167).

Fig. 166   By the spring of 2011, the overall structure of the tree had been completed.

Fig. 167   What the tree looked like in the early spring of 2012.

Fig. 168   What the tree looked like in 2012 when new leaves appeared.

Fig. 169   In the autumn of 2012, new leaves grew out after the old leaves were removed.

Fig. 170   What the tree looked like in the winter of 2012.

In late August 2012, all the leaves were removed and the tree was appropriately trimmed. A month later, new leaves grew out, small and neat. Everything was now ready for the appreciation of the red leaves in winter (figs. 168 and 169).

Fig. 171   In the winter of 2012, the tree was fully trimmed after the leaves fell.

Fig. 172   What the tree looked like after the leaves were removed in the autumn of 2014.

Fig. 173   The tree was moved into a specially shaped pottery container in 2015.

Fig. 174   What the tree looked like in the autumn of 2015 when new leaves came out.

When winter came, the leaves turned a colorful and intoxicating red. When all the leaves had fallen, the tree was fully trimmed one more time. The branches were clear and smooth and the whole work was dynamic and charming. It looked like a dancing forest or ten thousand horses galloping (figs. 170 to 172).

Since the original container was regular in shape, which did not match the tree in style and also affected the representation of the landscape, in the spring of 2015, the designer custom-made a specially shaped container to solve these problems (figs. 173 and 174 and see fig. 175 on page 104).

Fig. 175　What *Dancing Mountain Forest* looked like when the leaves turned red in the early winter of 2015.

Care and Maintenance

Ordinarily, the trident maple should be put in a moist place with good ventilation and sunlight. In summer, it should be slightly covered from the sun. In winter, keep in mind that it is cold-resistant.

During the growing period in spring and summer, the soil should be kept slightly moist. In autumn, when the leaves turn red and growth slows, the soil should be kept slightly dry. In the growing season, fertilizer should be applied regularly, but in small amounts. The soil should be replaced every two to three years before the tree buds in spring and after the leaves fall in autumn.

Redundant long branches and overgrown weak branches can be cut at any time. The tree should be trimmed every winter.

The diseases the tree is susceptible to include powdery mildew; common pests include longhorn beetles, slug moths, bagmoths and scale insects.

6. *Listening to Spring Water*

Tree species: five-needle pine
Type of rock: Yingde stone
Tree height: 150 cm
Designer: Zhou Qijin

This work consists of five-needle pines and some Yingde stones artistically organized together. It is a typical water and land forest penjing.

The five-needle pine has bold branches, dense leaves, and short needles. It is green year-round and is a precious penjing tree species. The nine five-needle pines in this work vary in height and thickness. Before being assembled, they had been bred for many years, but not shaped.

In early 2002, all the trees were initially shaped by wiring. The trunks, which were consistent in style, were mainly straight, but oblique where appropriate (fig. 176). All the trees were moved into one container for continuous breeding.

In arranging the trees, the designer followed the basic principle of penjing composition. The primary tree was arranged about one-third of the way from the right side of the container. Then the secondary and supplementary trees were arranged. During this process, special care must be taken with variables like tree height, density, location, etc.

After one year of growth, the trees were further processed. Some of the rigid branches were adjusted with a clamp bender to make them coordinate with other trees in posture (fig. 177).

Later, based on their growth, the trees were adjusted slightly every year. Redundant branches that affected the tree shape were cut. The cuts were sealed with healing agent in time to prevent the resin from draining.

In the autumn of 2007, when the leaves gradually became frondent, the trees were moved into a shallow container for

Fig. 176   In early 2002, all the trees were arranged together after wiring and breeding continued.

Fig. 177   In early 2003, some tree trunks with rigid lines were adjusted with a clamp bender.

Fig. 178   In the autumn of 2007, the plants were moved into a shallow container and breeding continued.

continuous cultivation (fig. 178). They were moved into a even shallower container in the winter of 2009 (see fig. 179 on page 106).

To maintain the shapes of the pines, the buds should be pinched off between March and April each year before new buds grow into needles. Generally, a pair of buds are left on each branch and one-third to two-thirds of their length should be removed based on their overall length

Fig. 179   In the winter of 2009, the plants were moved into a different, shallower container.

Fig. 180   In the early spring of 2016, the work was converted into a water and land forest penjing. The primary tree was arranged first, then the secondary and supplementary trees.

Fig. 181   The layout of the trees remained the same as before.

and growth. More can be picked of bigger buds and less of smaller buds. Similarly, more can be picked if the bud grows vigorously and less can be picked if it grows poorly.

In order to enhance its expressiveness, in the early spring of 2016, the creator converted the work into a water and land penjing.

The new marble container, 150 cm in length, is 30 cm longer than the original container. This extra length makes it possible to have more water and empty space in the work.

In making the water and land penjing, the location of the trees was first determined. The primary tree was arranged initially, followed by the secondary and supplementary trees. The layout of the trees was essentially the same as before. Only some slight adjustments were made in accordance with the representation of space and the water surface (figs. 180 and 181).

After the trees were arranged, the creator continued to position the rocks. First, rocks were used to make a slope bank, which separated the water and land. Then, the ornamental rocks were positioned on land and finally on the water surface. The rocks were arranged so that they created an undulating effect and coordinated well amongst themselves and with the trees. The coastline was winding and varied. Ornamental rocks were important to the treatment of the terrain and to the uneven water surface. Those in the water varied in size and density; those on land echoed with the bank and complemented the trees well (figs. 183 and 184).

To make the rocks fit with the bottom of the container, the creator cut their undersides flat with a stonecutter (fig. 182).

After the rocks were arranged, they were fixed onto the container with concrete and then soil was added to the container. The trees were moved into the container and the mosses were spread on the soil surface. The work was complete (fig. 185 and see fig. 186 on pages 108 and 109).

Fig. 183   After the layout of the trees was determined, the rocks were arranged.

Fig. 184   All the rocks in place.

Fig. 182   The rocks placed in water or used as slopes must be flattened at the bottom.

Fig. 185   By March 2016, *Listening to Spring Water* was complete.

Care and Maintenance

Five-needle pines love sunlight and are cold-tolerant. Most of the time, they should be arranged in moist places with good sunlight and ventilation. They should not be exposed to the scorching sun in summer.

The soil should often be moistened but also kept slightly dry. Fertilizer should be applied during the growing season. The soil should be replaced once every three to four years between February and March or in late autumn.

In spring, before the new buds grow into needles, about half of them should be picked. Trim the pine every winter.

Prevalent diseases include rust and root rot. Common pests are mainly scale insects, aphids, spider mites, etc.

Fig. 186   What *Listening to Spring Water* looked like in the early spring of 2020.

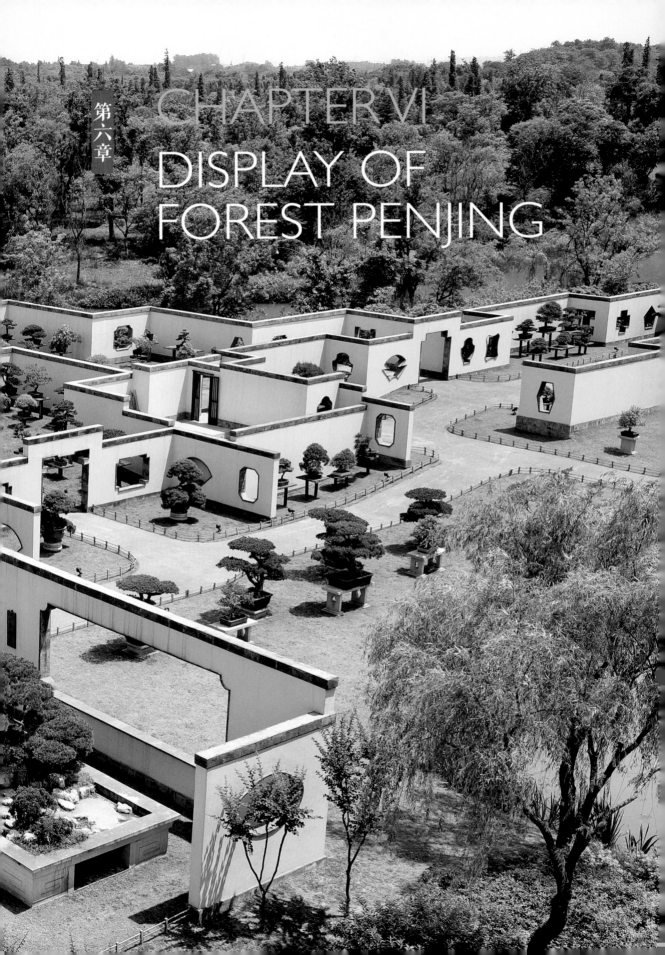

CHAPTER VI

第六章

DISPLAY OF
FOREST PENJING

A forest penjing can be understood as a three-dimensional landscape painting. It should be arranged carefully and artistically in a specific environment for the best viewing effect.

Generally, the container should be arranged slightly below eye level so that viewers can have a complete picture of the whole work. Depending on the environment or function, penjing can be displayed either outdoors or indoors.

1. Outdoor Display

A forest penjing is a living work of art. The plants cannot survive without sunlight and air. Therefore, works of forest penjing are best arranged in an outdoor environment with sufficient sunlight and good ventilation.

Outdoor places that house forest penjing include penjing gardens (fig. 187), parks, family courtyards, and other outdoor spaces. In addition, some large-scale penjing exhibitions are also held outdoors.

Outdoor display is mostly long-term. Therefore, the environment chosen should have good ventilation and sunlight and should meet the requirements for plant protection in summer and winter. Plants with different habits are best arranged separately. In winter, they should be kept out of the cold and in summer kept away from the sun. Since different regions have different climates, adjustments should be made based on local conditions. In addition, consideration should also be given to convenience in plant care and maintenance.

Forest penjing of different specifications can be displayed outdoors in appropriate spaces. If the space is too large, it will dwarf

On pages 110–111
Fig. 187   Exhibits outside the Yangzhou Penjing Museum.

the work; if the space is too small, the work will look cramped. A large space can be divided into many smaller spaces with walls to enable the viewer to observe the large within the small. Extra-large penjing works should be arranged appropriately in larger places so that they can be viewed either from a distance or from up close.

Since a forest penjing has only one major face for appreciation, works should normally be arranged against a background wall with the front of the work facing viewers. The background wall should be a single, neutral color so as to make the work stand out. A work of forest penjing can also be arranged against the wall of a building. In case a background wall is not available, the surrounding environment should be kept clean and tidy—otherwise, it may divert the viewer's attention.

Outdoor frames normally stand on the ground and are made of stone (fig. 188), antiseptic wood (fig. 189), concrete, or metal.

Fig. 188   An outdoor stone frame.

Fig. 189   An outdoor antiseptic wood frame.

Fig. 190   Forest penjing arranged together in a penjing garden.

They are usually waterproof, durable, and long lasting. Sometimes, the frames can also be piled up with bricks.

In a penjing garden, works of forest penjing can be arranged together or in intervals with other types of penjing. They should differ in height and be rich in variety (figs. 190 and 191).

In an outdoor penjing exhibition, specific exhibition stands are often erected. These should be 60 to 80 cm in height, with a clean background board behind them.

Penjing works arranged in family courtyards or outdoor public places are meant mainly for decoration. Therefore, they should coordinate with their settings and be convenient to appreciate, maintain and manage.

Fig. 191   Forest penjing arranged at intervals with other types of penjing.

2. Indoor Display

Forest penjing can be arranged indoors at home, in exhibition halls, or in indoor public places. Such a display is often short-term.

Penjing works cannot be installed indoors for long, especially during growing season, because the poor ventilation and lack of sunlight inhibit their growth. They can be rotated with outdoor penjing works on a regular basis. To help the plants grow, the length of time a work can be arranged indoors should be determined according to the season and the habits of different tree species.

Penjing works arranged indoors should coordinate with their setting in size, color, and location. Only in this way can they become objects of appreciation and elevate the beauty of their environment at the same time.

Indoor frames are either set on the floor or on a table. They are usually made of wood or bamboo. Floor frames, normally about 80 cm

Fig. 192   An indoor floor frame.

Fig. 194   A four-piece table frame set for rectangular containers.

Fig. 193   A table frame.

Fig. 195   A four-piece table frame set for oval containers.

Fig. 196   A naturally-shaped burl wood board.

Fig. 197 *A Peaceful Harbor*
Tree species: Chinese sweet plum
Type of rock: turtle grain stone
Container length: 150 cm
Designer: Zheng Yongtai
This water and land forest penjing is too big for a single frame. Thus, a four-piece table frame set was used.

in height, are arranged directly on the floor for medium-sized forest penjing (fig. 192). Table frames are usually very short and small and are mostly made of hard wood. They are arranged on tables or booths, upon which works of penjing are placed (fig. 193).

A table frame for forest penjing usually consists of four pieces (fig. 197) and is used either for a rectangular (fig. 194) or an oval container (fig. 195). It is ideal for various specifications of penjing works. A naturally-shaped burl wood board is often used instead of a frame for a forest consisting of a single tree with multiple trunks (fig. 196).

A forest penjing arranged at home is often displayed against the wall in the living room on a floor frame. Works of calligraphy and painting can be hung on the wall to complement it. A little work of forest penjing can be arranged on a small frame and placed on a table.

In an indoor penjing exhibition or professional penjing exhibition hall, forest penjing are often mixed with other types of penjing works (see fig. 199 on page 116). At an indoor penjing exhibition, the forest penjing chosen should coordinate well with the overall setting, and each of the individual

Fig. 198   The light-colored Chinese landscape painting in the background helps bring out the poetic and picturesque qualities of the work.

Fig. 199   At an indoor penjing exhibition, forest penjing are arranged with other types of penjing.

works should be highlighted. Here, penjing works are the priority and are complemented by the setting, a hierarchy that cannot be reversed. Normally, specific exhibition booths are set up for the works, in which small frames or floor frames are placed. A single light color or a quiet landscape painting should be adopted as the background, which can help bring out the poetic and picturesque splendor of the penjing (fig. 198).